HAUNTED
SNOHOMISH

HAUNTED
SNOHOMISH

DEBORAH CUYLE

Haunted America

Published by Haunted America
A Division of The History Press
Charleston, SC
www.historypress.net

Cover image: The Oxford Saloon, one of the most notoriously haunted buildings on First Street in Snohomish, is said to house eighteen or more ghosts! *Author's collection.*

First published 2016

Manufactured in the United States

ISBN 978.1.46713.697.6

Library of Congress Control Number: 2016939311

CONTENTS

Preface   7
Acknowledgements   11
Introduction   13

The Oxford Pool Room and Saloon   23
The Cabbage Patch Restaurant   31
The Carnegie Building and the Snohomish Public Library   37
The Marks Building and the Old County Jail   43
Haunted Historic Snohomish   49
Haunted Houses and Buildings in Snohomish   71
Fiddlers Bluff and Kenwanda Golf Course   81
The Maltby Cemetery, the Snohomish Pioneer Cemetery
    and GAR Cemetery   85
The Railroad and Lumber Mill Tragedies   97
The Snohomish River   113

Sources   121
About the Author   125

PREFACE

This book project is for my love of Snohomish, the town that has become my home for almost two decades and hopefully more decades to come. I love all the lore and legends, ghosts and spirits stories that people have told me over the years. It is fun to walk the streets today, the same streets Snohomish pioneers once walked, and think of how it was back in the old days. The stories here have been told to me by locals—some embellished over the years in order to make them more fascinating, I am sure, and some of the names in the stories have been changed to protect the innocent (or guilty?)—all told out of fun for the love of history, hauntings and lore. The book is not intended to be a nonfiction project, and with research, sometimes there are conflicting dates and facts in historic records. Please take it for what it is, a book full of ghostly tales and interesting history of the small river town located north of Seattle and all of its wonderful historic buildings that house century-old spirits. Enjoy!

This book is dedicated to everyone who loves Snohomish as much as I do and to all the people out there who are curious about the afterlife. Being a NDE (near death experience) survivor, I am probably a little more open-minded than most people. That tends to happen to us survivors. Perhaps someday science can actually prove what really happens to us after we die, the eternal mystery, but until then, it is all just speculation. Religion and science may someday agree, and maybe not. I see both sides of the debate. There are too many unexplained things that happen to each of us to *not* entertain the idea of ghosts and the spirit world. I read somewhere that God or spirits do give us signs when we ask for them, but we as humans are too busy or close-minded to see them for what they are or acknowledge them when they happen.

While my mom struggled with terminal cancer, we made a pact that after she passed, if she disagreed on something she would make me smell cigarette smoke (which she knew I hated), and if she agreed, then it would be Jovan Musk perfume (which I also hated; my mother had a funny sense of humor.)

After my mom died, often times I would smell one or the other odors when asking for her advice, and I do not allow smoking in my house nor do they even sell that perfume anymore as far as I know. A few days after she died, I begged her to give me a sign that she was okay. After giving up on the probability of a sign, one afternoon I came home and was extremely depressed about losing her and decided to just sit on my deck in the sun. A white butterfly soon came and landed by me. Something made me stare

Possible ghost of Charles Lindbergh (1902–1974), American inventor, pilot, author and explorer. Photo taken at Palapala Ho'omau Church by his grave in Hawaii. *Author's collection.*

at it for a while. It didn't move or even desire to fly away. After what must have been ten minutes, I quietly asked, "Mom, is that you?" It hung around for some time. It would not leave even when I tried to shoo it away with my hand or a letter. For about a week, that butterfly just hung out on the deck with me until even my son wasn't surprised by its presence anymore. He said, "Remember, Mom, Grandma said that once she died she wanted to be free. Maybe being a butterfly makes her free from the cancer." That made me smile. The next day, the butterfly was gone, never to reappear. I think it was her saying goodbye and letting us know that she *was* okay.

I also dedicate this book to my incredible son, Dane Brown, who has always been my best friend and cohort in a passion for writing; to my wonderful Middy, who never complains when I am writing nonstop, even though a yummy dinner and cold cocktail are always waiting for me to share with him; and, last but not least, to my incredible and loving mom, Roxine, who always believed that I could do whatever I set my mind out to do.

As for personal ghost evidence, I have a story. On a recent trip to Hawaii, I took part in a tour bus drive, and one of the stops was at the Palapala Ho'omau Church on Maui. I wasn't really listening to the guide, as the historic church had beautiful horses by the parking lot that were begging for a petting or two. I took many photos of them and the old church. Although we were not allowed to go inside the building, I quickly took a snapshot of the interior as I walked by a window. We casually strolled the grounds for a bit, and then everyone piled back on the bus. When I was scrolling through the pictures on my camera, I noticed a strange apparition that appeared to be sitting in a church pew. As I zoomed in on the image, it looked like a male figure wearing a dark T-shirt over a long-sleeved thermal top and jeans.

The tour guide was telling a story about how the famous Charles Lindbergh (the first man to fly across the Atlantic Ocean) moved to Kipahulu in 1968. After being diagnosed with terminal cancer, he decided to forgo treatment and lived out his final days here, never wanting to leave Hawaii. He was buried there in 1974. When I got back to the hotel, I was interested in learning more about Lindbergh, so I did some research. It was very interesting to note that in a large number of photographs of Lindbergh in his glory years, he wore long white gloves that reached to his elbows. Is this the ghost of Charles Lindbergh? That photograph always makes me wonder. It could be a trick of light, but the coincidence is just too much to ignore.

Some things have to be believed to be seen.
—Ralph Hodgson

ACKNOWLEDGEMENTS

My gratitude goes out to Christen Thompson, Ryan Finn and all the other wonderful people who work for Arcadia Publishing and The History Press. Without their kindness, knowledge and extreme patience, many books would never get to print! I also want to thank the numerous hardworking volunteers, especially Chris Gee, at the Snohomish Historical Society. They spend countless hours documenting newspaper clippings, photographs, maps and a million other things so that the history of Snohomish is well preserved for future generations to enjoy. Nate Cushman at the Snohomish Library and David Dilgard at the Everett Public Library/Northwest Room should also be mentioned, as their names come up in almost every conversation about local history. Their passion for and knowledge of Snohomish is remarkable. Bill Betten of Snohomish should also be commended for his continuous efforts to maintain local Snohomish history and protect its future. All the people at Historic Downtown Snohomish also work very hard to protect and preserve our beautiful city. And a big thank-you goes to all the many open-minded neighbors and locals who told me their ghost stories in order for me to share them with you. (Some names of people and places have been changed to protect their identities. I hope readers will respect people's privacy and not disrupt anything or trespass on their property in their search for ghosts.)

INTRODUCTION

The quaint town of Snohomish, Washington, is known for its preserved historical beauty, wonderful shopping and restaurants, friendly people and, some say, the many haunted buildings. Old architectural designs from the late 1800s are nestled in between a few modern ones, packed tight on First Street, and those that survived the tragic fire in 1911; they remain almost frozen in time. The nearby Snohomish River constantly threatens to flood the area—sometimes claiming lives of livestock and often forcing some people from their homes over the years—but Snohomish locals persevere and together fight the complications of living next to such an unpredictable river.

People visit from all over to enjoy a quiet day of antique shopping, great food, fabulous boutiques, live music and local art, as well as partaking in the many festivals, events, parades and farmers' market booths. For a small town, it holds its own when it comes to creating a unique and thriving atmosphere for several hundred thousand visitors to enjoy each year.

When one strolls the sidewalks today, moving in and out of the historic buildings, it is fun to imagine what life must have been like back then—the old times of horse carriages, top hats, corsets, five-cent drinks, locomotives sternly ordered to travel at just six miles per hour and a pound of tea costing just thirty-five cents. In 1864, the first road tax was implemented and was only two dollars.

Before 1871, the rutted paths called "roads" were basically just cleared areas chopped through the woods, winding through the tall trees and

Third and Union in 1859. "In the center is the Vestal house (228 Union) with the Gittelson home (223 A). St. John's Episcopal Church is left and First Presbyterian Church right." *Pettersen Family Collection, David Dilgard, Everett Public Library, Northwest Room.*

Historic Snohomish, then Cadyville, in 1900. From Third and Avenue C, pioneers cut trails from cabins to neighbors' homes to the river, creating roads. *Pett7, David Dilgard, Everett Public Library, Northwest Room.*

running between twelve and sixteen feet wide. Many so-called roads were so rough and primitive that they could only be traveled by foot. Later, when roadways were more accommodating and automobile travel a little more common, there were more cars on the roads. More cars did not mean more careful drivers. It was reported in the January 1938 issue of the *Snohomish County Tribune* that a tally of 239 auto wrecks had occurred the year before—apparently there were no drivers' education classes offered at that time?

Inside the shops today on First Street, the original hardwood floors carry deep grooves, scuff marks and sometimes even bullet holes in the walls that all have an interesting tale or two, if only voices from the past could tell them. Perhaps that is why the ghosts of Snohomish's past linger casually around town—so that their stories can finally be told?

Once a prolific river town, boats would slowly drift inward where bars, hotels and restaurants were waiting for them. Weary sailors, locals and hardworking policemen often shared the muddy streets of the town once named Cadyville. Large steamships would slowly drift up the canal along with smaller fishing boats. Snohomish was originally founded in about 1858 by Emory C. Ferguson, E.F. Cady and several others. The early pioneer

A handsome man in front of the "Stop and Shop," which boasts a sign reading, "American made bread—made here every day." *Snohomish Historical Society, BU-066.*

Auction signs read: "Farm, 29 acres, water, modern house, dairy barn," "Pasture for rent" and "10-20 McCormick tractor" for sale. *Snohomish Historical Society, BU-082.*

named Edson Cady named the spot when registering a post office. Cadyville changed its name to Snohomish in 1871. The first settlers here were mostly middle-aged bachelors. During its early years, an ambitious builder and architect named J.S. White was responsible for most of the gorgeous buildings during that time. His incredible architecture still draws interested crowds today, and the Snohomish Historical Society occasionally hosts informational tours charting his delightful work.

These two eager and early Snohomish pioneers, E.C. Ferguson and E.F. Cady, realized that the development of the Military Road (that promised to connect the two United States fort bases located at Steilacoom and Bellingham) was significant to the city of Snohomish. This road would someday become a real highway with the help of the government, and the point where it crossed the Snohomish River could be an excellent point of trade. With this new knowledge and great foresight, two other men (Egbert Tucker and Heil Barnes) joined Cady in the quest and quickly filed claims to the land near this intersection point.

Inside this variety store, a sign reads, "Chicken Dinner .05 cents." It also offers rubber goods, a public telephone and a few stools where customers can enjoy a soda fountain. *Snohomish Historical Society, BU-065.*

Buildings show addresses of 917, 919 and 923. Written below 919 is the name "Fred Schott," and below 923 is "Ben Barnes." *Snohomish Historical Society, BU-079.*

Ferguson was eager to file the first plat map in Snohomish in June 1871, providing numbers for the streets (First, Second, Third and Union), as well as four avenues (A, B, C and D). Later, in April 1872, the Sinclairs' plat provided the parallel streets named Commercial, May, Cedar, Maple, State, Willow and Alder. The little town was becoming organized and quite charming to locals and visitors alike.

But Snohomish hasn't always been as fortunate as it is today. In the 1800s, the town suffered a horrible spread of smallpox and, with it, a very high death rate that quickly claimed many lives, distilled dread and created panic in the town's survivors. It is reported that nearby cities quarantined Snohomish citizens from their towns for fear of the deadly disease. Yet like most towns in the late 1800s, there were some murders, a little mayhem, several interesting affairs, frustrating politics, typical bootlegging, possible "working girls," a few town drunks and everything in between.

The ghosts of some of those less fortunate supposedly still haunt their favorite places, like the Oxford Saloon (hosting up to eighteen ghosts, including a stabbed policeman named Henry), the underground county jail cells and the creepy confines nearby where Washington's first embalmer experimented his new practice on corpses. Ask many current business owners if they think their building is haunted and you'll rarely find any hesitation as they begin their tales of moving objects, eerie faces caught in photographs, the faint cries of invisible women and the stifled, heated arguments from male apparitions.

Steamer *Marguerite*, circa 1907. The bridge is the original one built to accommodate steamers. Postcard postmarked May 24, 1907, at Snohomish, Washington. *Snohomish Historical Society.*

The Snohomish River was one of the biggest draws of living in town. The boats could transport almost everything easily, especially when roads in early Snohomish were scarce and heavily treed. *Bill Betten.*

In several of the local pubs, frightened waitresses still get grabbed by cold, unseen hands as they work the tables. Some business owners seek out guidance from paranormal investigators and priests in the hopes of obtaining relief from these unwanted spirits, but the wandering souls of the dead do not want to leave their lovely town. Why would they? Paranormal investigators claim that traumatic events can somehow "trap" a spirit's emotions, which in turn can cause the misguided deceased to continue to haunt the place or person who created it. Whether or not ghosts are real is not the subject of this book and certainly a personal belief. It is sometimes hard to discount strange experiences that cannot be explained logically, leaving one's mind to wander.

Ghosts stories, legends and folklore exist in any town—big or small, new or old—as human beings are fascinated with the afterlife and are eager to capture "proof" of the spirit world. Apparitions are the most common form of paranormal activity. An animal or a person that keeps reappearing at a location over and over again is classified as an actual "haunting." An important characteristic of a classic haunting is noises. These noises imitate the sounds of human and animal activities, such as crying, chairs moving, dishes breaking and dogs barking.

Above: First Street looking west. A tailor, a photographer, a bakery and the Union Building are shown from Union. *Snohomish Historical Society, FS-003.*

Below: The same street view in 2016. In 1901, the first automobile came to town, owned by Lew Paramore, a Snohomish druggist, and it was a one-cylinder wonder. *Author's collection.*

Another form of activity is called the "crisis apparition." These are single events that typically occur when a living person undergoes a crisis and a loved one appears to offer them comfort in time of need. These crisis apparitions are commonly shrugged off as daydreams or ignored and labeled as strange flukes caused by stress. With all the tragedies Snohomish citizens suffered, crisis apparitions would seem most likely.

There are some common Snohomish legends of ghosts and haunted lore. At a nearby golf course, the dancing spirit of Wanda is seen on the eighth hole, her flowing dress caught from the corner of one's eye. When one walks

First Avenue, looking east, Snohomish, Washington, 1920. *J.A. Juleen Collection, J489, David Dilgard, Everett Public Library, Northwest Room.*

the train tracks, the faint music from a fiddle can sometimes be heard, the remnants of a lonely, miserable man who committed suicide on a hillside now termed "Fiddlers Bluff." A former schoolteacher and librarian named Catherine McMurchy from the 1920s still refuses to stop shelving books in the old Carnegie Building Library—creating such a stir in town, in fact, that she received her very own ghostbusting webcam.

The little town of Snohomish is loaded with fascinating history and many stories.

THE OXFORD POOL ROOM AND SALOON

The Oxford Saloon, located at 913 First Street, is considered the most haunted public building in the town of Snohomish. It is located in the Downtown Historic District. This beautiful building was designed and built by J.S. White in 1900. It was formerly called Blackman's Dry Goods Store, and since then, although it has changed hands several times, "Oxford" has always been included in the name. Apparently it cost Blackman $5,000 to build it in 1889. The Oxford was not used as a saloon until World War II. Just two years before the Oxford Saloon was built, a Seattle banker named James Furth opened the first bank in town, located nearby in the Cathcart Building. In 1888, it became the First National Bank of Snohomish and moved to the first brick building in town (and the county).

J.S. White was a prominent businessman and very talented architect in early Snohomish, and many of his buildings still stand today for people to admire. His unique style can often be pointed out, and the town conducts occasional tours of its great collection of historical buildings. The Everett Public Library also has programs that offer interesting details about White and his role in the development of early Snohomish. One wonders if the spirit of the man who loved Snohomish so much still wanders the streets today, admiring his beautiful, well-maintained buildings.

The Oxford has three levels. It is said that the upstairs portion of the Oxford Saloon was once run as a fancy bordello by a businesswoman named Kathleen or Katherine. Other locals say that the upstairs at the Oxford was never really a "bordello" but simply a card room where gamblers and

People say that the Oxford was once a bordello run by Kathleen and that a working girl was found dead upstairs. Others claim that the upstairs was never a bordello but merely a card room where people could have fun and play games. *Author's collection.*

women could play a hand or two. Now, just what the men did with their winnings is another thing. Katherine did not frequent the saloon but instead kept her office at a nearby Eagles Lodge. For some reason, she eventually did move her office upstairs in the Oxford. Perhaps to keep a better eye on her working girls? The stories about the Oxford's history might just be rumors and speculation, but the fact that many feel it is haunted is very real.

Many paranormal groups have investigated the Oxford and have determined that there are three ghosts upstairs in the current offices. One is a gentleman often seen in a bowler hat, a hard felt hat with a rounded brim that was popular with the working class in those days. Maybe this is the spirit of the murdered policeman Henry in his evening garb, eager to be relieved from his uniform? Or perhaps it is one of the many other ghosts said to haunt the Oxford. Policemen in the late 1800s earned a mere twenty dollars per month, with an additional two dollars for each arrest.

Two female figures are detected frequently upstairs in the Oxford building. The first is possibly the famed madam, often seen sporting a purple dress with purple bows. Many people visiting the offices say that they can catch the faint scent of her lavender perfume as it wafts lightly through the air. A second female figure is suggested to be an unwilling prostitute named Amelia, who worked for Katherine. Amelia's life ended tragically upstairs— her cold, dead body was found in her tiny closet in room 6. The details of her horrible death and the unconvicted murderer are not known, and it is also not clear whether poor Amelia was killed or committed suicide. Modern-day renters of the office that had once been known as room 6 report furniture being moved occasionally by unseen pranksters from the past.

A gigantic tin man hangs precariously from the ceiling, looming over patrons as they enjoy their music, food and drinks. The Oxford at 913 First Street is one of the most haunted buildings in Washington. *White Noise Paranormal Group.*

The creepy doll that is perched atop the bar has been known to wink at customers or move her arms as patrons enjoy their food and drinks. The Oxford may have as many as eighteen ghosts. The haunted doll was recently moved upstairs because it was "creeping people out." *White Noise Paranormal Group.*

The main section and restaurant of the Oxford has not changed much since the early 1900s, with its incredible multicolored glass windows and its grand false front. Façades were commonly used in the old days on commercial buildings to extend the look of the property and create a more impressive appearance to passersby in the hopes of enticing them in to order a beverage or dinner. Today, the interior of the Oxford displays many historical Snohomish photographs, which line the old wallpapered walls, and a mannequin of a woman dressed in a period piece hangs delicately from the ceiling, her face masked from view. Is she dressed up like Madame Katherine?

A gigantic metal tin man, strung west to east, towers over customers as they eat their food and enjoy their drinks. A dusty moose head still hangs above the bar, a tribute to days gone by; the huge mount can also be seen in old photos of the saloon. Out of spirit, the moose sometimes hosts a big red nose during the Christmas and holiday season. The original bar-back came from Cape Horn and is just as glorious today as it was back then. Thankfully, the brass spittoons have long since disappeared. There was an antique doll on top of the bar-back that reportedly closes her eyes now and then or winks casually at customers—creeping out locals and tourists who are trying to enjoy their food and drinks.

Here's a story from "M.D.," a thirty-year resident of Snohomish:

> *I don't believe in ghosts or spirits or any of that hogwash, but I have to tell you there has been a few things that have happened at the Oxford that make me disturbed and uncomfortable. One time I was in the bathroom downstairs washing my hands because we had just came from the garden and I had some stubborn dirt on them. For a second, I saw something move, not sure what. I felt that strange, tingling feeling down my spine. I looked down at my hands again, and then I swear I saw a face behind me. Could've just been the lighting, but it was very alarming. I quickly finished scrubbing my hands and got out of there as soon as I could. My wife said to me, "You feeling all right?" when I came back to our table. I said, "Yeah." but I must not have been too convincing because she bugged me until I told her what I thought I saw. She actually seemed relieved! I said, "Why, what's up?" and she said, "Oh my God, that has happened to me several times when we are here and I didn't want to tell you because I thought you'd laugh or tell me I had too much to drink."*

The downstairs segment of the saloon is often chained off during the week and is typically only open on the weekends. This is where a local legend tells of the horrible, fateful last night of a Snohomish officer of the law. In the 1890s, a local policeman named Henry met his untimely demise at the Oxford. Henry was a regular at the Oxford and occasionally worked as a bouncer for the tavern if things got a little out of hand. One night, he stepped in to break up a heated argument that led to a fight, and Henry unfortunately became the victim of the bloody stabbing that claimed his life. Many say that they see his spirit on the stairs as they descend down to the basement. Others feel a cold chill on their neck as they pass by, as if someone is reaching out for them. On the Oxford's website, there is a ghostly photograph posted in which an eerie face can be seen on the stairs. Is Henry still watching over the place? A black-and-white photograph hangs quietly at the top of the stairs in honor of him. Women report that they feel a ghostly presence while in the ladies' room. Could this also be Henry? Or could this be Katherine?

The Oxford today is always a favorite place to meet up and offers live music, dancing, great food and more. *Author's collection.*

Here is a local story from Ed, who lives in Cathcart:

I go to the Oxford because it's got good music and burgers and close to home. I typically just sit at the bar when I go there so I don't take up a table; it's just me. So I was sitting at the bar one night having a rum, and when I looked up, that ugly doll that sits up there on the bar moved. Maybe I was just seeing things or a car went by and the headlights hit it or something. So I ignored it and finished my drink. I kept looking up at the doll, though, waiting for it to move again. It didn't move, but it did close one of its eyes. That was enough for me. I still go there but keep my back to the bar. I don't like ghosts.

Here is a story about the Oxford basement:

I was downstairs at the Oxford playing pool and drinking with my friends. I always get a weird feeling down my back when I am there but ignore it. Last summer, I was shooting pool with my buddies and my phone rang. The reception isn't the best down there, so I said, "Hey, I'll be right back" to my pals and headed upstairs to go outside so I could hear better. As I was turning the corner at the base of the stairs to head up, I felt one of my buddies grab

28

An officer named Henry lost his life at the Oxford while trying to break up a bar fight. Some say that his restless spirit still haunts the Oxford and still protects the innocent. *Snohomish Historical Society, PO-002.*

the back of my shirt. I turned to see what he wanted…but my buddies were still over by the pool table, and the rest of the people were over by the darts. I don't really know what happened, but it surely felt like someone grabbed my shirt. As I headed on up the stairs, I felt it again. Dang! It took everything out of me not to run up those stairs and get outta there! I know my buddies would make fun of me if I told them this story. I am hoping it happens to them soon!

Who is grabbing people at the Oxford? Is it the ghost of the policeman Henry? Or maybe it is Madame Katherine making sure the ladies' skirts and blouses are presented just right for the paying customers? The Oxford has been investigated by many paranormal groups and psychics and also been featured in television programs. It is still considered one of the most haunted locations in Washington State. It is so notoriously haunted, in fact, that Zak Bagans, Nick Groff, Billy Tolley, Aaron Goodwin and Jay Wasley, the crew from *The Ghost Adventures* television program, came to Snohomish and investigated the Oxford Saloon in the summer of 2015.

THE CABBAGE PATCH RESTAURANT

The Cabbage Patch Restaurant on Avenue A is a local favorite and has experienced several tragedies, but it still thrives and is considered as haunted as the Oxford Saloon. The original house was built in 1905, and before becoming a restaurant in 1975, it was a private residence, a hair salon, a boardinghouse and even an antique store. Sondra McCutchan became the new owner in 1978, and the restaurant grew from just thirteen tables to a fabulous place that can hold a large number of patrons throughout its various themed rooms. On April 9, 2004, the Cabbage Patch caught fire around midnight, and it took forty firefighters and seven engine trucks to control the blaze. There are so many fires in Snohomish's history; it is possible that malevolent spirits might be at work causing havoc in town.

Here is a ghost story from "MS":

> *I was a breakfast cook at the Cabbage Patch, and like every morning, I came in and opened, getting everything prepped for breakfast, just like every other morning. I heard giggling and saw a young girl run over by our pie case, and I figured our baker at the time had brought her daughter to work, a rather normal occurrence. I decided to have some fun, so I snuck over to the case, jumped out and let out a loud "Rawwr…" No one was there. Freaked out, I went back to work, only to jump out of my skin five minutes later when the baker showed and shut the pie case, making a loud noise.*

Here's another story, as told by an employee of the Cabbage Patch:

Before the fire, the Cabbage Patch had a bar upstairs complete with an old-style jukebox. The staff had to unplug the box and drape the cord over the top every night before they left. That night, while our employee was sitting in the office, the jukebox started to play music. The employee ran out of the office to find the box off and the plug draped over the front. Needless to say, the book work was not finished that night, and the employee never came into the restaurant alone again.

Decorated with dressmakers' mannequins that display vintage hats and dresses, the Cabbage Patch is an adorable and comfortable spot to enjoy a nice glass of wine, the famed Millionaire Pie or dinner. The Garden Room, the Library Lounge, the beautiful bar with a breathtaking stained-glass window and the upstairs Fireside Lounge all invite guests to relax, unwind and stay for a spell. This place is so comfortable that even the dead don't want to leave it.

The Cabbage Patch before the fire on April 9, 2004. A female spirit named Sybil Sibley who died when she tripped down a staircase and broke her neck may still haunt it. *Joan Pinney of Joan Pinney Watercolors.*

The Cabbage Patch Restaurant at 111 Avenue A offers ghosts of a little girl, two gentlemen and a medium-sized dog, all of which have been seen loitering around the premises. *Author's collection.*

One of the most notorious spirits haunting the Cabbage Patch is an eleven-year-old, dark-haired girl named Sybil Sibley, who met her tragic death when she unfortunately tripped and fell down a staircase and broke her neck. Employees, customers and visitors have all reported seeing a young girl pacing the upstairs area, looking longingly out the window or floating on the stairwell dressed in white. Research discloses that Sybil actually died sometime in 1930, but apparently she missed her family so much that she followed them to their Snohomish home in 1954. Patrons today often trip on the last few stairs down the staircase and feel a cold chill as they carefully descend the stairs. Could Sybil's spirit be angry, confused or both? Is the touch of her hand a kindly offer of assistance so no one else endures such a tragic demise, or is it a slight push out of frustration? No one will ever know.

Here is another story from a Cabbage Patch employee:

The story of Sybil goes back to before the house became a restaurant. Staff and guests would report seeing apparitions of a young girl in a blue dress or hear the sounds of a child. The legend of Sybil varies but goes something like this. In the mid- to early 1900s, a family with a young girl lived in the house along with the girl's uncle, who lived upstairs. The uncle was known locally as a very angry man with a drinking problem. One day, the uncle got very angry with Sybil and pushed her down the stairs, breaking her neck. We have had several customers trip over the second to last step, the step she tripped down. A notable story with Sybil takes place in one of the houses up the street from the restaurant. A young boy used to play with Sybil in their backyard. The boy's mother questioned her son on his new playmate, and he had told her that Sybil hurt her neck falling down the stairs and lived in the Cabbage Patch. The mother couldn't see anyone, but her son could.

It is said that Sybil's not-so-nice uncle also haunts the Cabbage Patch Restaurant. Psychics have reported the presence of a sandy-haired male wearing a dark jacket that frightens poor Sybil. They thought that perhaps she was afraid of this man and did not fall down the stairs by accident at all. No wonder she is angry!

Here's another story from an employee:

Until a couple of years ago, a common sight in our downstairs bathroom was a face print that would form on the mirror. It became maddening to our staff, as they would clean the mirror and leave the restroom, only to come back to see the face staring at them. The face was noted by staff for over twenty years, until five years ago, when the face simply vanished. In the bathroom upstairs, we have an antique machine that was used to give women permanents. The "curlers" device will sometimes be moving as someone enters the bathroom (the door is kept closed, and no window is open), the old-fashioned curlers dangling, slowly moving back and forth as if they had just been taken out of someone's hair.

The scary-looking machine that is in the upstairs restroom at the Cabbage Patch was invented in 1905 by German hairdresser Karl Nessler. It became popular in the 1940s. The heated curlers would be applied to the person's head, and disgustingly, a mixture of cow urine and water was used as a curling solution. These curlers are often found swaying back and forth inside the bathroom. Could a female sprit eager to get her hair groomed for an upcoming party be playing with the old machine?

The owner and employees sometimes encounter another type of spirit, one of a furry companion. A phantom collie hangs around the kitchen, and

This page: This machine was used to give ladies curls in the 1940s. It is found inside the upstairs bathroom and often sways as if just removed from a woman's hair. *Cabbage Patch Restaurant.*

people feel his side brushing up against their legs as they work. Rumor says that it is Sybil's dog refusing to leave her side to this day. Or does he hang around the kitchen hoping for a few wonderful scraps?

Here is a story about a little old lady and her dog, told by "KK," employee at the Cabbage Patch:

> *The old back porch that was converted into our back room is home to two ghosts, an older lady and her terrier dog. Sometimes guests hear a dog bark, or more commonly, they feel paws on their legs. It is very common for employees in the kitchen to think they see an animal scurrying about the kitchen. When I started baking, it was in the summer and the kitchen was really hot. I propped the back door open to try and cool the room off and didn't think much of it until about an hour before I was done. I saw something small run right by me. My first thought was, "Oh no, I let in a raccoon or something since the door is open." I looked everywhere for the "animal" I saw and never found it. Finally, at 3:00 a.m., I was exhausted and decided to go home. I left a note for the cook and locked up. No animal was ever found. I later found out that it was common for employees in the kitchen to see this, and it was the "ghost dog."*

Sybil's rude uncle has some competition when it comes to male ghosts loitering around near the Cabbage Patch Restaurant. Nearby, a red-haired man with a long moustache bustles here and there, making his rounds and stopping in at the building next door, which was once used as a retail shop and then a restaurant and bar that played live music and had comedy shows. Perhaps the night life is more exciting to the ghost, which they call "Chester Billington." Psychic investigators Russ and Sandy Wells from the Paranormal Research and Investigations team experienced many strange phenomena at the Cabbage Patch while staying there. Sandy felt a sharp pain in her head and concluded that Chester "possibly died from a blow or gunshot wound to the head." Russ felt that Chester had been stationed in "the Pacific Theater during World War II on an island held by the Japanese." Both investigators felt that Chester's ghostly spirit had returned to Snohomish to be close to his family. He continues to stroll up and down Avenue A to this day, popping in and out of the buildings there, happy to be back in Snohomish.

The Carnegie Building and the Snohomish Public Library

The grand building known as the Carnegie Public Library in Snohomish was built in 1910 and still stands today; it is just one of the thirty-two remaining historic Carnegie Library buildings left in the state of Washington. A woman named Emma C. Patric was the town's first librarian in 1901. It is now the oldest remaining public building in the city and is under a proposed remodel in order to bring the building back to its former glory. Its mission is to gather enough donations to create the Carnegie Educational Center, a Place for Families, which will honor the intent of the original Carnegie Library Building. Carnegie libraries are legends in themselves, and their significance can often be overlooked. These grand buildings were built with money from Andrew Carnegie; an incredible 2,509 Carnegie libraries were built between 1883 and 1929. By 1919, there were 3,500 libraries built in the United States alone, with the funding for construction paid by Carnegie grants.

The Carnegie Library in Snohomish cost more than $10,000 to build back then. In 1903, the ambitious women of the Cosmopolitan Club, dedicated to child welfare and literature, teamed up with the Hui Wa Wa club and formed a library association. It was their brainstorm to try to allocate this Carnegie Library donation.

The building in Snohomish was once a thriving library but today is in need of repair and restoration. After multiple reports of a woman's shadowy image being seen at the library, the *Herald* newspaper teamed up with the Friends of the Snohomish Library in 2002 and installed a webcam, or shall we call it a ghostcam?

The Carnegie Library was built in 1910. It is haunted by the spirit of a librarian named Catherine that strolls the halls still re-shelving books in her dress and hat. She died in 1956. *Snohomish Historical Society, BU-085; CC BY-SA 3.0.*

The beautiful carved motif above the door reads, "The gift of Andrew Carnegie, Snohomish Public Library." Will the ghost of Catherine stay? *White Noise Paranormal Group; CC BY-SA 3.0.*

The beautiful carved motif above the door at the Carnegie Library Building reads, "The gift of Andrew Carnegie, Snohomish Public Library." Some say that they see the image of a woman's face peeking out from the upstairs window, looking out over the courtyard area. When the addition was an art gallery, many employees saw a dark shadow image walking through the halls and into the various parts of the building.

Here is a story from an anonymous person who used to work in the library when it was an art gallery:

The addition to the Carnegie was an art gallery for some time. I don't know how many times I thought a customer had walked into the room, so I would stop what I was doing to address them with a "Hello! Welcome to our gallery!" only to discover no one was there. Then, of course, I would get a cold chill and a very creepy feeling up my spine. It took everything out of me to finish my shift! At other times, works or supplies would be moved about without any of us doing it. Now, I know we can all misplace things and not remember, but in an art gallery you have to be more careful to never touch or move another artist's things. There was also an apparition I would see out of

Catherine earned her own ghostly webcam. She had no gravestone, so locals purchased one for her. She rests at Evergreen-Washelli Cemetery, and her tombstone reads, "Cherished Snohomish Librarian." *White Noise Paranormal Group.*

Modern view from Avenue C in 2016, with the Annie's on First and Cathouse Pizza businesses. *Author's collection.*

the corner of my eye that seemed to be an older gentleman wearing suspenders, [with] *a long beard and overalls that were too short. He did not give me a creepy or scary feeling at all—more like a warm, welcoming feeling.*

Catherine worked at the library from 1923 to 1939 and apparently liked to wear the color blue. Most reports of her presence have centered on the heavy, dark-stained staff room doors upstairs, and all reports have been peaceful rather than frightening. She lived in the town of Snohomish with her sister until 1950. After her passing, it was noted that she had no grave marker, since there was no money in her estate, so concerned citizens did some fundraising and raised enough money to purchase a gravestone for her. The cemetery donated a black stone, and others raised $410 to engrave a white lily, a book and her epitaph.

Paranormal activity surrounds the upstairs level of the Carnegie, but reports have also been made for the stairs leading down to the lower level. Catherine suffered great personal loss in her lifetime, as her parents and all three of her siblings died here in town. Although their bodies were taken

Emma Patric and Catherine McMurchy posing in the Snohomish Library in about 1950. *John Patric and Everett Public Library.*

back to North Dakota for final burial, perhaps their spirits stayed here in Snohomish, thus keeping Catherine's spirit here, too.

The locals welcome and embrace Catherine's friendly spirit, and if she feels more at home in the old Carnegie Building, they will all just let her remain there. Perhaps one day the Carnegie Building will open back up, and Catherine can get back to work.

THE MARKS BUILDING AND THE OLD COUNTY JAIL

The Marks Building, located at 1024–26 First Street, was originally built in 1888 and ran as John Otten's Dry Goods Store. The story is repeated that Mr. Otten unfortunately fell behind on his payments, and a local real estate investor, Tom Marks, repossessed the building and soon had his name carved in the stone entryway. In earlier times, it is reported that there were two entrances—one for men and another for the ladies.

Later, it was the courthouse and jail, and the large downstairs area is now partially remodeled and up to date. The south/street side of the basement areas still have the solid stone arches that were once impenetrable jail cells and the thick purple glass circles that once cast the only sunlight prisoners were allowed to enjoy. From the sidewalks above, the small purple glass circles look almost like decorative accents rather than the long-ago signs of an underground jail holding criminals. There was another building attached to the Marks Building that earlier burned down. After the big fire in 1911, the town decided that it would be wise to build with bricks in the future.

The Marks Building has a metal cast plaque on the west outside corner wall that boasts the building's original name, as well as touting the fact that it housed the "first flush toilet in Snohomish." Marks served as the city clerk in 1910, and the members of the council joined in his building for the meetings. Not too long after the town of Snohomish incorporated, the city funds took a turn for the worse, and it is rumored that meals for the prisoners were not supplied unless the providers received cash up front.

Snohomish police often had their hands full with problems and people who had a little too much to drink. During this time, Everett was a dry town, so thirsty patrons flocked to Snohomish to enjoy a few libations and have a good time. There were many saloons in town over the years: Saloon Dubuque (1891), the Quiet Place, the New Brewery Saloon, the Ivy Saloon, the Palace Saloon, the Portland Saloon, the Chicago Saloon, the Depot Saloon, the Great Northern Saloon and the Gold Leaf Saloon (where the notorious 1895 murder of William Kinney by William Wroth occurred on First Street), just to name a few.

One interesting first case found in the Snohomish County records is against Jacob Brem, who was charged with assault and intent to commit murder. He was found guilty and sentenced to "two months additional imprisonment and sentenced to pay a fine of $5." A Judge Lewis of that time was determined to set an example to murderers, thieves and vagabonds.

At the old Snohomish Jail in the basement of the Marks Building, it has been noted that unexplained groans can be heard like someone is in pain—not surprising, since many of the pioneers had been jailed after a night of drinking and the all-too-occasional bar fight. There have also been many reports of a chill that would briefly take over the room without any reasonable explanation.

The Marks Building at 1024 was built by Tom Marks in 1888. The town was at a population of about seven hundred and included a sawmill turning out twenty thousand board feet of lumber daily, six saloons, one church, two skating rinks, three lawyers and two doctors. *Author's collection.*

Left: The Marks Building boasted the "first flush toilet in Snohomish" In 1907, the population of Snohomish was about two thousand residents. *Author's collection.*

Below: The Marks, seen from the river between Avenues B and C after the 1911 fire. Downstairs, the old jail cell arches are still evident. Prisoners would receive light through the purple glass squares in the sidewalk seen from above. *Snohomish Historical Society FI-009 and FI-011.*

Most reported paranormal activity encountered at this site are noises that sound like heavy metal keys jangling and loud bangs that sound like someone hitting metal against the wall. Could these be ghostly residual sounds of hungry prisoners demanding attention as they eagerly waited for their food? The keys could be the sounds of the heavy key rings the prison guards used to carry to open the jail cells. Or maybe it is "Omaha Bill," still angry about being locked up for the murder of "Texas Jack" back in 1895.

There are also reports from building tenants of the locked elevator moving to different floors with no one operating it, as well as people seeing apparitions of an old woman sitting in a rocking chair.

STORIES FROM EMPLOYEES AND TENANTS IN THE MARKS BUILDING

Here is a story from "J.":

> *There are locks on the third-floor elevator, yet one night the elevator door just kept opening even though it was* locked. *I checked it after the first time to make sure that it was locked. Every time it happened, my dog's hair would stand straight up and she would go crazy. My dog has been coming to work with me for years, and I had never experienced that before. I used to stay late a lot after work, but after that, when weird things would happen, it was time to go home! LOL! I knew of another tenant who refused to stay here after 6:00 p.m. unless someone else was here. He was completely freaked out. He never told me what spooked him…*

Here is one from Mark of Snohomish:

> *I had an office downstairs, and I would work on projects there. I don't know how many times I would turn to see a woman sitting in an old rocking chair just watching me. The first time I saw her I thought she had accidentally come down the stairs, got tired and decided to sit for a spell. I turned to set my tools down, and when I turned back around, she was gone! I looked for her but couldn't find her. I just figured she made her way somehow back up the stairs (even though it would have been impossible to move that fast at her age). I am not a believer in ghosts and such, but after I saw this woman multiple times, I realized there must be*

more to this supernatural stuff than I previously thought. I know I am not crazy. After a while, I just said "hello" to her when I saw her out of the corner of my eye.

Here is another from "DC":

We used to count our money for the day and do bookwork in the basement. One time I was counting the money, and it kept "changing" on me, like someone was fooling around or playing a joke, but no one else was there. I would count the change, go to write it down, and when I looked again, the coins would clearly be wrong…so I would count it again…and again. After a few times, I said out loud, "Ok, enough already! I want to go home, I'm tired!" The coin thief stopped. Another time I was doing books and saw a man walk past my door. There was supposed to be no one else down there, but once in a while, someone would out of curiosity. I got up to tell them, "Hey, you can't be down here," but there was no one there. It scared me, so I went back into my office and locked the door. After a few minutes, I was getting a very uncomfortable feeling, almost a panicky, "fight or flight" feeling. All of a sudden I just had *to get out of there. I quickly grabbed my things and started to make my exit. As I turned to lock my office, I heard what sounded like the clunky jail cell keys jiggling—like the ones the old wardens would carry for each of the cells. I ignored it and started up the stairs. About the fourth step, I heard a loud* BANG! *like someone smacking something against the wall. Needless to say I ran so fast up those stairs my heart was racing by the time I got to the top. From that day forward, I never went down there without my black lab Bonnie at my side for protection!*

HAUNTED HISTORIC SNOHOMISH

Life for early settlers wasn't easy. The constant threat of disease was a daily battle. Felling the large timbers was extremely dangerous. Children worked, and their daily chores started before the sun even rose. Boys would chop wood for the stove or fireplace, water and feed the animals, tend to the garden and do other jobs. Young girls would milk cows and gather eggs, make breads and butter, wash laundry and make candles and clothes. Land was cheap back then compared to today. In 1862, there was a program called the Homestead Act, which required people to reside on and improve the land for five years. The land could also be purchased from the government after six months for a mere $1.25 per acre. As for the town, Mr. Ferguson arrived in Cadyville in 1864 with his wife and child. He built a tiny building (Snohomish's first business) on the corner of Cedar and Commercial Streets. Later, in 1871, Mr. Ferguson decided to draw out the town's streets in map form—from Union to Avenue D and from First Street to Fourth Street. A year later, the Sinclairs (who came to Snohomish in 1864) also recorded the streets and focused on the eastern section parallel to the river, numbered east to west from Union Avenue. In 1892, a pound of ham cost just $0.14 and a pound of tea just $0.35.

Some early settlers started businesses right away, as it was convenient for travelers to come by boat to the little town of Cadyville. One of the early pioneers of Snohomish was Mr. Charles Bakeman, who died in his home on Avenue B at the ripe old age of ninety-two in September 1952. He was born on October 26, 1860, in Wisconsin. Bakeman left his home at age

Early settlers of Snohomish in 1892. The average price on a claim of 160 acres of land was $500 in 1882. *David Dilgard, Everett Public Library, Northwest Room.*

twenty-two to head out west and traveled all the way to Portland and then Seattle. On a boat trip he took in 1883, he took a liking to the little town of Snohomish and decided to move there. He started a furniture business in town that thrived for many years. Bakeman had a desire to make a horse buggy, so he did. This was one of the first ever to be made in the area. Since there were no good roads at the time, his buggy did not offer much use. A man from the nearby town of Monroe liked the buggy and promptly gave Bakemen $120 for it.

In 1884, the Snohomish River froze, causing quite a bit of concern. This single event changed the course of Bakeman's life and steered him into the direction of undertaking. With a frozen river, there was no way for boats to transport anything or anyone—including a recently deceased person. Since Charles was in the furniture business, soon he was asked to make a casket for the deceased individual.

Unwillingly, Mr. Bakeman had to make the casket and perform the dreadful task of undertaking. Charles became the first funeral director in Snohomish County and one of the first embalmers and coroners in the state of Washington until he sold his practice in 1934. Charles married Ms. Nina Blackman, from the prominent Blackman Brothers Mill family. He then became a mayor and city councilman. Upon Bakeman's death, he was buried at the local GAR Cemetery in the outskirts of town.

Early settlers of Snohomish. Six men, one woman and two dogs pose. *David Dilgard, Everett Public Library, Northwest Room.*

A board and lodging restaurant around 1892, with a group of early business-minded pioneers. *David Dilgard, Everett Public Library, Northwest Room.*

The Pioneer Hotel, operating in 1892 with an early, rustic group of people gathered around it. Notice the two men perched casually on the roof of the porch. *David Dilgard, Everett Public Library, Northwest Room.*

Early pioneers were eager to expand the town and put down residences. Hardworking people were drawn to Snohomish not only for its beauty but also for its location by the river, which made it even more satisfying to live there. Although many people were an integral part of the making of Snohomish, three names surface time and time again when the history of downtown is researched. Blackman (the three brothers Arthur, Hyrcanus and Elhanan), Ferguson and Cathcart. Together they conquered many issues and were very active in making Snohomish a better community.

When Snohomish incorporated in April 1888, these men were part of it, listed as the top three trustees (H. Blackman). When the proposal of an electric light plant (called the Snohomish Electric Light Company) was developed, these men again were listed, as president (E. Blackman), vice-president (Ferguson) and treasurer (Cathcart). When a branch of the American Building and Loan Association was opened in Snohomish, the officers were A. Blackman as president and Ferguson as vice-president.

The energetic Hyrcanus Blackman built a skating rink in 1881 on the corner of B and First that he later tore down in 1886 to make way for his beautiful three-story, four-star Penobscot Hotel (destroyed in the 1911 fire) that charged $1.50 per room. The Penobscot Hotel was designed to be the most magnificent hotel the residents of the city (and county) had ever seen. It measured forty by one hundred feet in size, claimed that 50 percent of the

FIRST STREET LOOKING EAST SNOHOMISH WASH

First Street in the 1900s, showing the Cathcart Building, built in 1876 and rebuilt in 1910 (now Hoity Toity). The Brunswick Hotel makes up the apartments upstairs, and a bridal dress shop, the Twin Eagles Café, Fresh Salon, Grow Washington and Worthy are below. *Snohomish Historical Society, BU-001.*

rooms were actually "heated with stoves" and bore the name Penobscot in raised gold letters. It officially opened on May 23, 1888. He rebuilt the site after the 1911 fire using architect J.S. White, creating a two-story building using brick and concrete to avoid any future fire disasters.

Today, this "Burns Block" building houses Bee Bops & Lollipops (1112 First), Victoria Village Antiques (1106 First), Piccadilly Circus English Pub (1104 First) and the Cin-a-mon Stik (1102 First).

The Annie's garden boutique at 1210 First Street used to be a furniture store and undertaking business. Cathouse Pizza is located next door, and the three-story brick building was Burns Block, built in 1890 by White. This brick building is responsible for stopping the horrific fire in 1911 from destroying the remaining buildings on the north side of First Street heading west.

Here is one tale from the author:

> *I helped decorate the old building at 1120 First Street (now Cathouse Pizza), and I tell you what—so many strange and unexplained things! The previous owner would tell me that huge piles of tile would be moved over night when the place was empty. Voices heard while going down the stairs. I once heard a woman's voice as I descended the stairs, and at about*

This page: First Street looking east from Avenue C. The furniture and undertaking business was where Annie's is now (1210). There is also shown Schott's Pioneer Market building, a hardware store and Palace Restaurant (where the 1911 fire started). The horse carriage was used to transported both furniture and the deceased. *Snohomish Historical Society.*

the fourth step she called out a name. When I researched the name, it belonged to a woman who had lived there a long time ago. Was she bothered by the remodel? I have heard that spirits become more active if someone is remodeling or construction is going on, so that would make sense. Later, the owner at that time called me because his female employees were becoming scared. They felt they were getting grabbed on the wrists by an "invisible person." He asked me to come down and see if I felt anything creepy, so I went. I had a glass of wine and looked around but didn't feel anything out of the ordinary. He explained that some female employees were feeling like their wrists were being tied or something, and they would sometimes get strange marks on their hands as if the skin were being twisted. A little creeped out, I went home. About an hour later, I looked down at my hands, and the skin looked as if it had been twisted! Maybe it was just a coincidence, but I took a picture with my cellphone and sent it to the owner, asking if that is what the girls' hands looked like. He said, "Yes, exactly!" No matter how hard I rubbed my hands, soaked them in hot water or applied lotion, my hands remained that way for another couple of hours. I have no explanation whatsoever for what happened. I believe the owner went on to "cleanse" the building, and as far as I know, no new reports have been made to these effects. Hopefully whatever naughty spirit was in that building decided it was time to move on.

Historic Downtown Snohomish has been protected by local groups and organizations to preserve its beauty.

FRED'S RIVERTOWN ALEHOUSE

Fred's Rivertown Alehouse at 1114 First Street is a local hot spot for great food that offers a fantastic selection of various Scotches. It is always packed any time of the year, day or evening. At one time, the space was previously occupied and run as the Gem Saloon, but that building was destroyed in the horrific fire of 1911. At the time, it was owned by a man named Connelly, and the fire damage was estimated at $5,000. First Street property is limited, so the space was rebuilt after cleanup from the fire was finished.

It's not a very big place, but Fred's has some great character and unique charm. To think that for more than one hundred years, locals' and visitors' boots and shoes have been pounding the same section of land and bellying up to the bar for a cold drink or a game of cards. Employees today, when asked if they feel Fred's is haunted, will be quick to answer *yes*. Here is one story from a server at Fred's:

This place is for sure haunted. See these metal cups? They are on little hooks, and they are pretty hard for us to get off the hooks even when we need them to make drinks. They come flying off the hooks like someone is hitting them with their hand from behind! And our glasses are always being knocked off the shelves; that's why we have the chains across the front now, not that it really helps. Lots more strange stuff has happened around here. Even just today, the paper towel dispenser in the ladies' room would keep going off even though the door was closed and no one was in there. There is no reason for it to be doing that. There is a lot of unexplained activity in the kitchen area, too. It is the most haunted. People are always complaining about things being moved. Also, there's this metal grate thing out by the kitchen, and it makes a distinct sound when you step on it. A few times someone will be alone in here, and they hear that grate being stepped on as if someone is walking over it. No one is there.

When asked if they know the name of the ghost, there is a quick reply: "Harvey. We all feel it is Harvey. And not just because Harvey is a big name in town. In fact, we don't even call it that. We call the ghost 'the Peeker' because to us it seems like he is always peeking around the corner, peeking into rooms, peeking in and out of places."

Did original pioneer John Harvey, who died in Snohomish in 1886, frequent this spot after work? Was it possibly his favorite hangout or a place to meet with friends? Is he really the one haunting the modern-day Fred's Alehouse?

After a very dangerous and adventurous life prior to coming to Snohomish (at one point he risked death), John Harvey purchased a section of a land claim along the south side of the river near town for fifty dollars and built a small log cabin there. In 1861, Harvey, along with pioneers E.C. Ferguson and Henry McClurg, worked on the board of county commissioners. Harvey married Christine Noble, and they had the first white boy born in Snohomish County in 1873. They named him Noble George Harvey. John Harvey was a great hunter and often supplied meat to the local restaurants and hotels. Noble grew up to own the first Ford automobile in Snohomish. The Harvey family now operates Harvey Airfield and the Snohomish Flying Service.

Here is one story about Fred's from a local named Sara:

I work down the street in town and go to Fred's afterwards to have a drink or two and unwind. Although it is my favorite place, at times I feel like someone is watching me, especially when I am heading to the bathroom and am in the little hall area. One time it felt like something grabbed my side, and I thought maybe my sweater got caught on something somehow, but when I turned, no one and nothing was there and my sweater was fine. On the way back to my barstool, I felt it again. There has been plenty of times things like this have happened there. I hear stories of it being haunted. I knew another gal who worked there, and she always felt like she was being watched. One time, she told me she was cleaning up the bar area late at night and a glass came right off the shelf and crashed. She just cleaned it up but found it weird that a heavy glass would just move like that. Who knows.

STAR CENTER MALL AND ANTIQUES AND THE OLD COLLECTOR'S CHOICE RESTAURANT

Star Center Antique Mall is located on the corner of Second and Glen just next to Historic First Street. The building was rebuilt in 1982 and has a menacing ghost or two lurking about. On several occasions, there have been sightings in the basement, where the restrooms are located. One customer told of seeing someone enter the ladies' room ahead of her, and when she got inside, there was nobody else in there. Throughout the mall, lights will flicker even though there are no electrical issues in the building. A bartender who used to work in the restaurant on the main floor also had several experiences when closing up at night. Feeling like she was being watched while mopping the floor, she would look up to see a distinct shadow out of the corner of her eye. There were also a few occasions when something touched the back of her neck—like a finger sweeping across her hairline.

THE 1895 MURDER OF WILLIAM "TEXAS JACK" KINNEY BY WILLIAM "OMAHA BILL" WROTH

It was well past midnight on a cold evening in October at the Gold Leaf Saloon on First Street in 1895. The owner and bartender, "Omaha Bill," in a very drunken state, pulled his pistol and shot "Texas Jack" in a Wild West–style shootout. Wroth was promptly arrested for the murder and locked up in the city jail.

The Gold Leaf Saloon had a reputation for being too disorderly, and 677 concerned citizens complained and requested its license to be revoked. But when it came before council, the petition was rejected, and the saloon remained open. Maybe the citizens were right? If the Gold Leaf had been closed, perhaps Texas Jack would have lived longer.

As reported in *The Eye* newspaper and *Snohomish County Tribune* on November 1, 1895:

> *This morning sometime between 1 and 3 o'clock, Wm. Wroth, alias "Omaha Bill," shot and killed William Kinney, also known as "Texas Jack," at the front door of the Gold Leaf saloon. Texas Jack, who has been working in a logging camp east of here, came to town last evening, made some purchases and then proceeded to load up with fire water, and resorted to the Gold Leaf. Wm. Wroth, who lately became a co-partner with Della Stone, the proprietor of the Golden Leaf, tends bar at that resort nights, and it seems often imbibes himself. Between Wroth and Kinney there had been a standing feud and this was aggravated last night by the liquor both had imbibed. After a good deal of hot words, Wroth threatened shooting, and Kinney not departing, he carried out his threat, firing three shots, the second of which struck Kinney and pierced his heart. He staggered about fourty feet from the door and fell dead. The officers were called and arrested Wroth, and he is now in the county jail. Coroner Rogers came up this morning and this afternoon summoned Messrs. Warner, Whitfield, Cole, Foss, Boyle and Spurrell to sit as a jury of inquest, which is listening to testimony as the Tribune goes to press.*

James Sipprell, the arresting officer, had his hands full with angry and intoxicated Wroth as he tossed him in the city lockup to cool down and sober up. Wroth (Omaha Bill) was later acquitted on the ground of "justifiable homicide."

With so many bars lined along First Street, it is amazing there weren't more murders committed while patrons were intoxicated. Rumors have it that at some political events, eager candidates often provided free liquor in the hopes of gaining votes. Does the angry spirit of Texas Jack still roam the nighttime streets of Snohomish in search of Omaha Bill, hoping to get revenge for his murder?

OTHER HAUNTED SPOTS

The Oxford isn't the only building reported to be haunted in the Historic District. The building located at 1107 First Street, now called Snohomish Bicycles, is said to have had creepy experiences down in the basement. The events were very active during the time the building was used as the Pizza Palace.

Here's a creepy story told by Lisa, a former employee of the Pizza Palace:

The restaurant mostly just used the basement for storage and junk; the walk-in cooler was down there for perishables, beer, that kind of stuff. The bar and pizza was upstairs, on the second level and out back on the deck. I never got any bad vibes while upstairs working, but after one or two times downstairs, I would refuse to go down or find an excuse not to go down there. And if I did have to go down there, I would walk about as fast as I could—I'd just basically grab my things and bolt back up. After just a couple months working there, I refused to go down there at all by myself after what happened to me. Here's how my scary story goes...

We needed to fill the beer fridges behind the bar before we opened. So I start taking inventory of what I needed to bring back up. Of course, a person

Many eerie stories are told about this building, now a wonderful bicycle shop. During an earlier remodel into the Pizza Palace, many objects would be moved. When it was opened as a restaurant, staff often reported being touched and an overall really creepy feeling in the basement. *Author's collection.*

Antiques are a huge part of Snohomish's charm. Many local shops offer thousands of old items for sale. Could these relics retain paranormal energy from previous owners? *Snohomish Historical Society BU-059.*

can only carry so much, so I had to make a few trips. First trip down, nothing creepy. Second trip down, I started to get the feeling someone was watching me or that maybe someone was hiding down there. There was a back door that led out to the riverside, but we kept it locked at all times so no one would really be able to get in, but you never know. I kinda looked around the huge room to see if anyone else was down there. I called out, "Hello?" No one answered. I continued my trip to the walk-in cooler…fast. I was inside and gathering the beer I needed to pack back up. I propped the cooler door open because I have a fear of being locked inside by mistake. I do this at any place I work that has a walk-in cooler. I am a little claustrophobic. Anyway, I propped the door open with a beer box and was counting bottles and going through my list when the cooler door slammed shut!

I freaked out. I immediately jumped over the boxes and pushed on the heavy door. It opened right up. The beer box I used was pretty heavy and couldn't be easily moved, so I figured it was a co-worker who was just messing with me for a joke. I yelled out, "NOT funny!" as I was pretty mad at whoever thought that it was funny to shut me inside, but no one was there. It was about twenty or thirty feet to the stairs that led back up to the main area, so I would have seen someone running back after closing the door, I am pretty sure. I looked around the basement, thinking maybe a co-worker was hiding from me. "Hello? Not funny, dude!" Again, no one responded. I went back upstairs. My boss was on the phone behind the bar. The other gal working was cleaning off tables and filling the shakers. As far as I know, no one else was on their shift yet. I didn't say anything to anyone because I didn't want them to make fun of me.

So…I guess I had to go back down and get the beer. I thought to myself, "It could have been the wind or maybe the box was not very secure"…you know the things you tell yourself when something like this happens. Anyway, back into the cooler, this time I made sure the door was propped open and there was no chance of it closing on me again. I started gathering the beer again. I kept one eye on the cooler door, but nothing happened. I packed as much as I could carry into a spare box and exited the cooler, kicking the door closed behind me. I made my way to the stairs with no problem. I did still feel like I was being watched, though. The worst part I remember was that just as I was about to take the first step back up, it felt like a hand grabbed the back of my neck. I just about dropped my box! I moved fast, as fast as I could carrying a heavy box up those stairs. The second thing I saw and felt was what appeared to me a person's arm reaching out of the air to grab at me, like it wanted to keep me down there with it. I actually saw an arm-appendage thing grabbing at me, the hand almost like a claw. I made my way up those stairs so fast, and I'll tell you my heart was pounding and I broke out into a cold sweat. My boss was like, "You ok?" I just shook my head. I will never get that image of that arm out of my head. I checked with a few other people that worked there, and they said the basement gave them the creeps, too.

VICTORIA VILLAGE ANTIQUE STORE ON FIRST STREET

This enormous antique store is filled to the brim with booth after booth of thousands of antiques and collectibles. When asked if the building was haunted, the owner simply said, "I'm not sure if I believe in that stuff, but I will tell you that countless times I have customers come back down from the upstairs. Some won't even go up there anymore, and they all tell me the same story. They say that there is a 'spirit up there that follows them around.' I find it interesting that so many people who do not know one another all tell me the same thing."

Egan and McGrath, Snohomish Studio and a few horse carts parked near present-day The Repp on the corner of Avenue A and First Street. *Snohomish Historical Society, BU-073.*

Who could this nosey ghost be? A deceased antiques lover? An old shop owner of a previous store? The hotel owner when the Penobscot Hotel thrived at the very same location? Or is the spirit a former customer who passed away and misses shopping at their favorite antiques store?

It is hard to tell who the spirit might be, but it is definitely busy, following patrons around through the cluttered aisles of fabulous artifacts from days gone by.

THE MURDER OF CHARLES SIEBERT

Lowell is a little town that exists just a few miles outside Snohomish. Incorporated in 1850, it is still an adorable city nestled near the river. But back in 1875, the gruesome murder and mutilation of a well-known sheriff plagued the small town and took Snohomish County by surprise. Sheriff Charles Siebert lived just outside Lowell and was savagely killed by his teenage son. Siebert was an active man in the county and well respected. His son, age nineteen when he committed the crime, escaped capture by the police. A chase followed, and he ended up being captured in Seattle and brought to trial. The young boy was acquitted on grounds of insanity.

Snohomish County had no jail at this time, and the expense of his capture, trial and care of the boy unfairly fell to the County of Kitsap. These expenditures depleted the county's funds quite rapidly. All unpaid taxes soon felt a 25 percent hit, and collections followed. The ghost of poor Siebert came back in another form months later—another court bill, to the tune of $508.25. A new tax levy came into play once again to help pay for it.

There are no legends of a ghost that haunts the streets of Lowell at this time, but the story is told so people can keep on the lookout for the spirit of a policeman near Lowell and Snohomish.

THE FIRES ON FIRST STREET

It is said that some poltergeists can move objects and create more noise than a common ghost. They are the scariest of all types of hauntings because it is believed that they can actually cause physical harm and damage. With so many fires igniting time and time again on First Street, it does make one wonder if there was possibly some sort of supernatural entity at work starting the flames. Logic would have it that business owners would become

Above and next page: The devastating fire of 1991 destroyed thirty-five buildings. Fire has plagued Snohomish many times over the years, even as recently as one that damaged the Cabbage Patch Restaurant in 2004. The Marks Building can be seen across the street. *Snohomish Historical Society, FI-015 and FI-012.*

more careful after the first fire (or two), and if poltergeists can cause havoc, then maybe that would be an explanation.

With all the fires, the Snohomish Fire Department was reorganized in 1890 and soon called itself Snohomish Engine Company No. 1. The city then spent another $85,000 on street improvements, which included the much-needed wood planking on First Street.

In the year 1893, a large number of fires affected Snohomish. On a cold night in January 1893, flames destroyed the Northern Saloon and

Another fire took hold of First Street on April 25, 1911. In this image, an Angels Beer sign at the Magnolia Tavern and the Eagle Café are visible. *Snohomish Historical Society, FI-002.*

barbershop, and the nearby Kirk Furniture Store was also damaged before the flames were brought under control. To the firefighters' surprise, the extreme cold weather had caused the fire hydrant to actually freeze, and it had to be quickly thawed by placing a barrel over it with a lit fire inside so they could pump water. After the complications of this fire, the city gave $1,400 to the fire department for better hoses, with two new carts, and included the addition of Hose Company No. 2.

Even with new equipment, when another fire broke out on July 10 the same year, the Bakeman Store was heavily damaged before the fire was extinguished. The odds must have been against the Bakeman Store, though, because just a few months later it burned to the ground. Rice & Gardners Meat Market and the upstairs offices were also destroyed in the fire. The losses were huge: Bakeman at $17,500, Rice & Gardner at $2,400, Doctor Keefe and Doctor McCain at $3,000, Coon at $1,000, Elwell at $250 and the Headlee & Headlee law library at $4,000, including the permanent destruction of all the municipal records. Flames were soon to start their path of destruction again, this time at Barrett's Liquor House, with a whopping loss of $16,000 in all.

Disaster struck once again on First Street on June 2, 1911, when an incredible blaze wiped out thirty-five businesses in town. The damages for the buildings was estimated at $150,000—a very hefty sum in those days.

This page: During the 1911 fire on First Street, many buildings were completely destroyed, most of which had little or no insurance to cover the damage. The Hotel Northern was located at 1120 First. Here firemen are struggling across from the present-day Annie's (1122 First) and Cathouse Pizza (1120 First) between Avenue B and Avenue C. The tall brick building (now Quilting Mayhem at 1118 First) saved them from burning, too. *Snohomish Historical Society.*

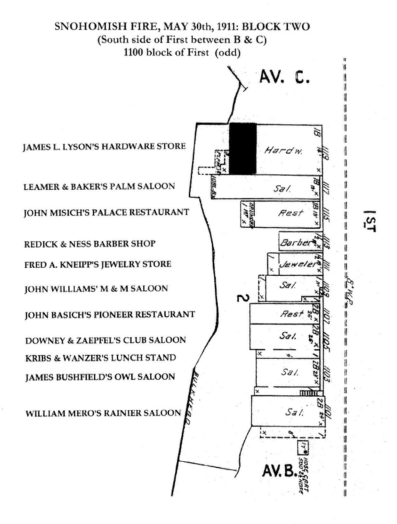

SNOHOMISH FIRE, MAY 30th, 1911: BLOCK TWO
(South side of First between B & C)
1100 block of First (odd)

This page and next: These hand-drawn Sanborn insurance maps from 1911 show the buildings marked by addresses and type of business. *David Dilgard, Everett Public Library, Northwest Room.*

The fire started in the downstairs of the Pioneer Restaurant (other articles claim it started in the Palace Café) and spread quickly. The larger of the damages were recorded as the Rainier Saloon (owned by Albert & Mero) $9,000, Owl Saloon (Bushfiled) $4,000, Club Saloon (Downey) $3,000, Club & Pioneer Building (Evans) at $4,000, M&M Saloon (Williams) at $1,300, M&M Building (McGuiness) at $1,500, Palace Restaurant (Misich)

SNOHOMISH FIRE, MAY 30th, 1911: BLOCK SEVEN
(North side of First between B & C)
1100 block of First (even)

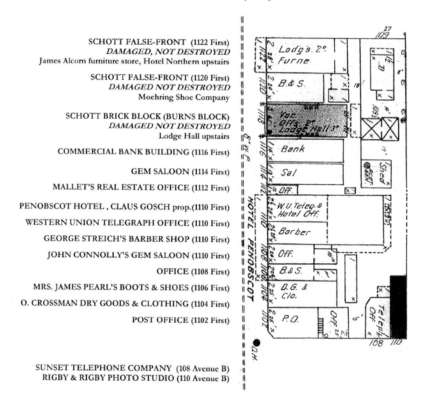

SCHOTT FALSE-FRONT (1122 First)
DAMAGED, NOT DESTROYED
James Alcorn furniture store, Hotel Northern upstairs

SCHOTT FALSE-FRONT (1120 First)
DAMAGED NOT DESTROYED
Moehring Shoe Company

SCHOTT BRICK BLOCK (BURNS BLOCK)
DAMAGED NOT DESTROYED
Lodge Hall upstairs

COMMERCIAL BANK BUILDING (1116 First)

GEM SALOON (1114 First)

MALLET'S REAL ESTATE OFFICE (1112 First)

PENOBSCOT HOTEL , CLAUS GOSCH prop.(1110 First)

WESTERN UNION TELEGRAPH OFFICE (1110 First)

GEORGE STREICH'S BARBER SHOP (1110 First)

JOHN CONNOLLY'S GEM SALOON (1110 First)

OFFICE (1108 First)

MRS. JAMES PEARL'S BOOTS & SHOES (1106 First)

O. CROSSMAN DRY GOODS & CLOTHING (1104 First)

POST OFFICE (1102 First)

SUNSET TELEPHONE COMPANY (108 Avenue B)
RIGBY & RIGBY PHOTO STUDIO (110 Avenue B)

at $2,500, FA Kneipp Jewelry Store at $6,000, Palm Saloon (Leamer and Baker) at $7,000, Palm Building (Harbers) at $3,000, JL Lyson Hardware Store at $12,000, the three-story frame Penobscot Hotel Building at $6,000, the Penobscot Hotel (Gosch) at $5,000, O. Crossman Dry Goods at $10,000, Gem Saloon (Connelly) at $5,000 and many more. Unfortunately for the buildings and business owners, only some had insurance; others had none at all. Interestingly enough, Pioneer Restaurant owner Billy Basich (whose building the fire started in) was listed among the dead until he sat down at a rival restaurant and ordered his breakfast.

From a hand-drawn map from May 30, 1911, the buildings are listed at that time as being on the north side of First between Avenue B and Avenue C: buildings spared by the fire included Annie's at 1122 First (then James Alcorn Furniture Store, an undertaking business, with the Hotel Northern upstairs), Cathouse Pizza at 1120 First (then the Mochring Shoe Company) and Quilting Mayhem at 1118 First (then the Schott Brick Building, with the Lodge Hall upstairs). This brick building was responsible for stopping the 1911 fire from destroying the remaining buildings listed eastward on First Street. (The flames were so hot during this fire that when remodeling the Cathouse Pizza building, scarring from the fire was found on parts of the structure.)

The buildings completely destroyed by the intense fire included 1116 First, the Commercial Bank Building; 1114 First, the Gem Saloon; and 1112 First, the Mallet's Real Estate Office. At 1110 First, there were several buildings and businesses listed: the Penobscot Hotel (Claus Gosch property), Western Union Telegraph Office, George Streich's Barber Shop and John Connolly's Saloon. At 1108 First, there was an unidentified office; 1106, Mrs. James Pearl's Boots & Shoes; 1104, O. Crossman Dry Goods & Clothing; and, finally, 1102, the post office. Andy's Fish House and a parking lot and the

A family stands in front of the H.F. Parks Grocery Store, getting ready to help patrons for the day. The address reads that it is located at "2225½" somewhere in town. They offered tobacco, fresh vegetables and a good selection of other necessary items. *Snohomish Historical Society, BU-067.*

Twenty-two men pose in front of the local IGA Store, part of the Snohomish Fruit Growers Association. *Snohomish Historical Society, BU-068.*

Legion building are located where these buildings once stood. Below is a beautiful riverside trail for walking or biking.

Although no deaths were reported from these fires, the trauma of such events can create crisis apparitions and hauntings. It took nine years to rebuild on the corner of Union and First Street, which was previously called the Cleveland Block. Edgar Wright decided to build a one-story structure that would soon be occupied by the Snohomish Furniture Company. In 1914, Feger's Bakery in town listed bread prices at just five cents per loaf and six loaves for twenty-five cents. Two loaves of two-day-old bread could be purchased for five cents, and doughnuts were just ten cents per dozen.

Haunted Houses and Buildings in Snohomish

There are many houses in Snohomish that people feel are haunted or occupied by restless spirits. Common occurrences in people's homes can sometimes be quickly explained away by faulty construction, loose hinges, various drafts and electrical issues. Other noises cannot be explained away or ignored. A puzzling factor is why some people are disturbed by these rappings and movements and others are not. Is it possible that some people have a more open mind to the spirit world or that the ghosts know they are willing to listen to them?

People have been mysteriously drawn to a particular room only to find what they have been searching for, as if a helpful guide led the way. Not all spirits create mayhem and disorder—some simply want to help or hang out.

The Old Goodwin Farmstead Off Broadway

Here is a story about a rapping noise from Rachel about a house in Snohomish near Kenwanda:

> Whenever I am at my mother-in-law's house in Snohomish, we sit and have coffee at her kitchen table. Soon a series of knocks comes from the refrigerator. We always joke that it is a leprechaun that wants out. To me it sounds almost like Morse code, and I am inclined to tape-record the

sounds and find someone who can decipher Morse code and see if there is a message! My mother-in-law was told that refrigerators make a similar noise when they are getting ready to crap out, so she went and replaced her tired fridge. Much to both our surprise, the refrigerator is still making the noise. Now I am more intrigued than ever to see if the raps create a message, but what if it is trying to tell us something scary? The house is one of the original structures and now over one hundred years old. Who knows what has gone on there over the years. Some things are better left unknown.

Here is a story from neighbor and friend Bryan:

Whenever I would visit this home, there was a particular presence I picked up on in the living room area. If we were watching television I would see, just out of the corner of my eye, what appeared to be a male figure wearing suspenders, a long beard and highwater jeans standing in the doorway with a big grin on his face. It seemed to me that he would be waving his hand in a friendly gesture, as if to say, "I'm here, look at me!" It got to where we would just ignore him, and he eventually just went away.

THE 1886 MAUGHLIN HOUSE ON FOURTH STREET

Rebecca Dickinson, the well-known children's book author, bought the town's most famous "haunted house on the hill" twenty-five years ago. In the late 1960s, the structure was being threatened with demolition by the city, as it had been vacant for so long. Windows were broken out, names were carved in walls and kids would party and hold séances there.

The legend is that the original home was lost at a poker game. The home went through several more owners until the Maughlin family purchased it. Locals tell of many ghost stories that surround the mansion's history, almost too many to tell, but no book about haunted Snohomish would be complete without the inclusion of Rebecca's mansion.

When one walks into the house, it is like stepping back in time and into another world. She has painstakingly remodeled, decorated, torn down, adjusted and added on to the structure for more than two decades.

Rebecca answered a for-sale ad that boasted a "bell tower that would be a perfect studio!" She quickly called about the home and then made an offer on it. The title closed on the purchase of her home on Halloween—that should have been an indicator. Her first night in her new home made

The haunted Maughlin House on Fourth features legends of a man hanging himself from the bell tower. *Rebecca Dickinson, from the Maughlin family.*

her question her plans for the new house. When she and her partner were downstairs measuring rooms and discussing remodeling ideas, they heard heavy footsteps upstairs. Worried there might be teenagers playing around, they went up to investigate. No one was up there. Strangely enough, they soon heard loud walking again, but now the footsteps were downstairs! Chills ran down both their spines. Not wanting to jump to conclusions, they carefully walked back down the stairs to the main level.

The porch door was open, and when they went out, they noticed that a light was on in the bell tower. "Did you turn on the light in the bell tower?" she asked her partner. "No," he replied. Just then, the door slammed shut, and her partner screamed. Rebecca had a moment where she thought to herself, "I actually *did* buy a haunted house!"

Later, she heard a rumor about a man being hanged in the bell tower, and there was another story of a young male being pushed to his death from the bell tower. Teenagers used a Ouija board and told her that it spelled out the name of a young girl and that she was in a "bad way" (pregnant); the couple had quarreled over it, and he accidentally fell from the bell tower. Rebecca often sees shadows of what appears to be two people struggling in the tower. Could this be the residual energy of the fight that claimed the young man's life?

When the home needed a new foundation, it required that the enormous building be jacked up in order to proceed. They had to remove a big cedar log that was rotten. Workers told her that there was a large wooden box under what was then the carriage house (now called her "monkey room" because it has beautiful wallpaper with monkeys on it). They couldn't access it because there was not enough room to get to it without complications. Rebecca didn't request they try to get the large box out.

There is an unusual and unexplained knocking sound that comes from the wall that separates the monkey room from the dining room. The large wooden box is located below this area of the home. She sometimes wonders if the box was an old coffin and if someone's remains are buried there. Could the knocking be a trapped soul wanting attention? Perhaps.

At times, her antique piano will play with no one at the keys. Rebecca reports feelings of someone watching her when she is alone in the house. She promptly tells them, "Stop watching me!," and they seem to oblige. Her favorite ghost story is from her sister, who is an engineer and does not believe in spirits:

> *The front door was the entry to the old payroll office, and Rebecca had it nailed shut until it could get fixed. I had my children there, and I was picking them up one night. She was going to leave the front door unlocked, but when I got there, Rebecca had possibly forgot because all the doors were locked. This was before the time of cellphones, so there was really no way to wake her up. I thought, "All the doors are locked. How am I going to get in to get my kids?" I walked around the house in the dark and was getting a little frustrated because I just wanted to get home with my children and sleep. When I came back around the side of the house where the front door was again, it was open. I figured Rebecca finally woke up and came down to unlock it for me, then went back to bed since it was so late. I was able to round everyone up, and off we went. The next day, I called Rebecca, and she said she never got up. Then she asked me, "So how did you get in?" I told her that when I came back around the house, the old payroll office door was open. She said, "Just a minute." Apparently, she went and checked the front door, and yes it was still nailed shut! I got goose bumps. But then we both decided that maybe it was just a friendly, motherly spirit who was helping out and opened the door so I could gather my children.*

Another time, her son was sitting in the room downstairs, and when he looked up, he saw a woman dressed in black walking up the stairs. She stopped midway, turned around, looked straight at him and then disappeared.

THE "I" HOUSE IN DOWNTOWN SNOHOMISH

Here is a story from Paul Williams:

> *In 2001, I had bought and was working on "I" House* [name changed to protect current owners], *the house on Avenue D that was built by a lumber baron. It's large, including a full basement and an attic that*

was used for dances and has a "secret" room that was used to hide alcohol during Prohibition. I had a lot of contractors on-site for about four solid months but often worked there late into the night by myself. Often, I felt I was not alone and was bothered enough at times that—even at fifty-one years old—I left the place quickly, not returning until the next day. The basement is partitioned into several rooms. One, on the east end, is a "cool room" that once served as a root cellar. It has old wooden shelves and has not been refurnished. In the center of the basement are two finished rooms, including one that contains the stairs leading up to the first floor of the house. The western end is dirt floored and contains a small workspace, the steam generator for the radiated heat in the house and the bottom of the dumbwaiter shaft that can be used to move small items from one floor to the next. This part of the basement is where I encountered the ghost.

On a sunlit day in April or May, there were several contractors on-site, working at various tasks such as repairing windows, putting plaster on bathroom walls and replacing some exterior wood that had dry-rotted. I was working on window sashes that day and went into the west end of the basement, where there was a supply of old window hardware. I entered the room through a small door and noted a man kneeling on the floor. As I walked past him, I said hi but kept moving because he was looking at me with a frown on his face and didn't appear happy. I got a chill as I passed him and turned to look back at him, but he was gone. He would have been no more than six feet from me at any time that I was in the room. The room was well lit because of windows and lights, and the only way out was the way I had entered, so it was not possible for him to exit without my seeing him do so. He just vanished.

I really believe I saw a ghost that day. I had been working with everyone on-site for months, so no one was a stranger to me. I'd never seen that guy before. And the eerie, chilling feeling that I got as I passed him was like nothing I had or have since experienced. I did walk out of the basement looking to see if I'd somehow missed his exit, but there was no one around, and people I asked said they'd seen no one leave the basement. The man looked to be around thirty to forty years old. He was thin, had dark-brown, thick hair combed back over his head on all three sides. He was well tanned, had on a dark-brown, buttoned shirt, with sleeves turned up. His pants were buckskin colored but looked like they were made of cotton, and he had on brown pull-on boots that looked new and expensive. I remember the details because the image I have of him is so vivid in my memory. I have always felt that he wanted me to look closely at where he had been kneeling,

*like perhaps there was something buried under that dirt floor. I never had
the nerve, honestly, to look. I left that house a few months later when I
divorced my wife, but I've never forgotten the encounter with the man in the
buckskin pants. I have occasionally thought about asking the current owners
if they've had any experiences that they found unsettling, but I don't know
them and don't think it would be appropriate. I also wonder if the man I
saw was a former owner. I was told that I was only the fourth owner of
the house since it was built, but I've never seen any pictures of the previous
owners. It would be interesting to investigate that.*

THE HAUNTED HOUSE IN DUTCH HILL

Here's a story from "DA":

*I bought a house in Snohomish off Dutch Hill about ten years back. I fell
in love with the house instantly, and we made a full-price offer on it before
even seeing the inside. I know that sounds ridiculous, but we couldn't help
ourselves. We had to have it! After moving in, things started to happen—not
necessarily scary but still a little frightening. Just a few months after the
purchase of the home, my husband and I starting arguing. His personality
seemed to change. We had been together for a decade, but once we moved
into the home, he started acting moody, at times violent and unpredictable—
traits that were not common before. I can't blame it all on the house, but
it was very odd. People that would come over also felt very uncomfortable,
especially in the kitchen and dining room area. The most interesting thing
I ever experienced was ongoing until the day I moved out. Whenever there
was tension between my husband and myself, I would hear what distinctly
sounded like a wine glass being set down on a counter just a little too hard.
Once I actually did it just to see if that was the sound I kept hearing, and
it was spot on! I can still hear that clank of a wine glass in my head.*

*I would wonder if maybe a woman that lived there before me (who
drank wine) would partake in a few glasses while her and her husband were
fighting, possibly drinking one too many glasses, and out of frustration or
hurt would plunk her wine glass down on the counter....I never felt scared
while living there, but many times I felt like I was not alone, even after he
moved out. Cold chills were common, but I blamed it on common drafts
in the big house and open rooms. The day before I moved out, I woke up*

suddenly and saw a strange black mass about the size of a beach ball at the end of my bed. It appeared to me like a million little bugs or something all huddled together to form this "ball." I rubbed my eyes, thinking my vision was blurry, but it didn't go away. As I watched it, it slowly moved toward me then gradually up toward the ceiling. I carefully followed its path with my eyes as it moved to the corner where the ceiling meets the wall behind the bed. I spotted a small box up there on a shelf that my husband had left. The black mass then slowly moved "through" the wall and disappeared. I just got up and left the room. To this day, I still wonder what was in that box and if the mass was trying to show me something that I needed to know or whatever. I guess now I will never know.

The House on Ninety-first South of Snohomish

Here is a story from Angela in Snohomish:

When we first moved into my house, I would always see shadows in the back hallway, like a person pacing back and forth. When I was in the living room, I would feel a very cold breeze. I would just feel like someone was standing by me, a presence of some sort. Later, I moved my mom in with us because she became ill. Many times I kept thinking someone was going into her bedroom to visit her, so I would go see and no one was in there with her. As she got sicker, she would always ask, "Who's that man sitting at the end of my bed?" I would ask her back, "I don't know, who is it, Mom? Is it Tom?" My brother, Tommy, was dead during this time. I then asked her, "What does he look like?" She told me he had a flannel shirt on, a baseball cap and was tall and thin. This apparition would sit at the end of my mom's bed every night. I still thought maybe it was brother, somehow wanting to comfort our mom, but she got mad at me and said, "No, don't you think I would know my own son?!" Then she would say, "Momma's gonna come and get me and take me home." I thought that my grandma was going to come and take her back to heaven with her, as it was getting close to "that time." A few weeks later (the night that my cousin was killed), I saw a mass of some sort swirling over my mom's bed behind her head. Nervously, I asked it, "Reveal yourself!" and all of a sudden I saw what appeared to be a beautiful angel over my mother's head. Then, as quickly as it appeared, it was gone. I didn't tell my mother about this because I was worried it might upset her.

About twenty minutes later, my home phone started ringing, and it was my sister calling to tell me our cousin Jerry (who was a deaf mute) was accidentally killed while crossing the road. He had a note he always kept in his pocket in case something happened to him that had my sister's phone number on it in case of an emergency. I guess the driver expected him to be able to hear the car coming, but of course he couldn't. I often wondered if the angel I saw was my cousin Jerry.

After my mom passed, I told the nun that came to pray for my mom what I saw, and she said, "That is such a gift to be able to see an angel. It was a blessing. A gift. Be thankful."

Later that year, a neighbor came over and was telling me how she used to ride her horse in my pasture and roller-skated in the basement of my house when she was a young girl. At that time, she was friends with a teenage boy named Doug who used to hang out here with her after school. She said he had accidentally overdosed from alcohol and pain pills at my house and died there in the basement. He had lost his mother, too. Remembering the male figure always at the end of my mom's bed, I asked her what this boy had looked like. What made my hair stand up is that the description of the boy she told me about matched the male figure my mom was seeing those few weeks before she passed on. He was a lanky teenage boy that always wore flannel shirts and a baseball cap.

I then had someone come in and bless my home. The only thing I feel is a cold breeze every now and then, which really could be anything. I do get comfort in the fact that the boy was kind enough and sat quietly by my mom's side in her final weeks. Perhaps he found comfort in being with my mom while she was alive since his was already gone.

THE SNOHOMISH SLAUGHTER AND RENDERING PLANT

The Thomas Family Farm off Highway 9 is a wonderful, haunting experience for all to enjoy. As the story goes from its website:

In 1935 the Snohomish Slaughter & Rendering Plant at 9010 Marsh Road was built by brothers Sam and Dean Thomas. The story tells of a major tragedy that occurred in 1975. Sam met his horrible and gruesome fate that took his life while working the meat plant. His body was quickly ripped in half by one of the meat grinders, and the upper half of his body was never found. Rumors suggest foul play; others say Sam just accidentally tripped and fell into the machine.

Locals claim that his angry spirit still haunts the building. Is Sam in search of his killer, or was it an accident and he is simply unable to move to the next dimension? Are these make-believe stories, exaggerated legends or the truth?

Upon investigation, there was a meatpacking business located in Snohomish west of Airport Way called the Columbia Packing Company. It was formed after World War I by a group of men in town and was run as a slaughterhouse; later, it processed meat products such as bacon, ham, wieners, sausage and bologna. It made products that were sugar-cured, a process it developed that differed from the typical salt curing process. It would also smoke the hams in a large smoker out back. Wages at the meat plant in the 1930s were reported to be ten dollars for six ten-hour days or sixty cents per hour.

Putting the historic tragedy behind it, today the Thomas Family Farm boasts a fantastic Zombie Safari Paintball Hayride (you get to shoot at live zombies!), the Nightmare on 9 Haunted House, a fun Flashlight Corn Maze F.S.I. (Farm Scene Investigation) event, fire pits, beer gardens, pumpkin patches, rides on monster trucks and a fun gemstone mining experience. Halloween events in town don't get much better than this.

Stalker Farms

Stalker Farms is located at 8705 Marsh Road and is one of the main fall haunted attractions in Snohomish. As stated on its website, it offers "Jed's Reckoning," a spin on a corn maze. The very scary event has everything: dolls' heads, bloody handprints, dark cornfields, clown faces and more. The corn maze plays off a story: "The Slasher family had a distant preacher cousin named Jebediah Slasher. He didn't get along with anyone who didn't share his beliefs in Samhain, the occult and corn….Over a century ago, during Halloween, Jebediah disappeared in the cornfield." Some say that he left to share his gospel, while others say that he was murdered. Strange rituals and noises can be heard coming from the large corn maze. If one is willing to walk through the eerie paths of spiders and corn stalks, they just might run into a ghost or two—or maybe Jebediah himself. These legends may just be hogwash, but where legends are concerned, no one really knows.

Stalker Farms also has another creepy attraction based on a clown story: Pogo the clown escaped to begin his own traveling show called Pogo's Playhouse. Rumor is that his first and last stop was Snohomish. Is Pogo really gone or just hiding for the opportune time to scare someone?

FIDDLERS BLUFF AND KENWANDA GOLF COURSE

FIDDLERS BLUFF

Fiddlers Bluff is a beautiful area with an incredible view of the Cascade Mountain Range just south of Snohomish and to the east of the Kenwanda area off Connelly Road, east of Highway 9. The steamships used to travel down the Snohomish River through the area on their way to Fall City for trade.

Here is a story by "MJ" of Fiddlers Bluff:

> *I bought a house several years ago near Fiddlers Bluff. I had heard the legends about the fiddler who killed himself, but I don't know if I believe those types of things. I will say that I often experienced the vision and strange presence of the spirit of a young boy in my house. I used to joke that he was playing hide-and-seek. Even the cleaning lady had made remarks about seeing what seemed like a young boy wearing short pants like jodhpurs and a hat similar to a golfing cap. When a friend moved in, they also commented on the strange "sightings" of a young lad, poking in and out of rooms and ducking behind couches and such. I didn't really give it much thought until I went to the bank here in town one day and there was this large old-time photograph behind the counter that was a group of people…and the children were wearing the type of clothes we all saw this boy wearing! I am curious if a young boy got killed by the train tracks when he was playing with his friends.*

Fiddlers Bluff, just east of the Kenwanda area south of Snohomish, as seen from Springhetti Road downhill and to the west of it. *Author's collection.*

I should do research, but maybe I don't want to know. It freaked me out a little.

Fiddlers Bluff also runs along the old Northern Pacific Railroad tracks, and its name is recognized among the county's first road districts in 1861. Dozens and dozens of road petitions and hearings were finally put into action, the first being to construct a district from Snohomish to Wood's Prairie. The second road district to be divided ran from Mukilteo to Snohomish, thus sectioning the county into two road districts. In 1862, more districts were formed, one being from Fiddlers Bluff to the forks of the Snohomish. All of these districts gradually grew until they reached the Stillaguamish in 1871 and out to the Sultan River in 1877.

Fiddlers Bluff today is well known for the legend of the "Miserable Fiddler":

At that very bluff, there was a depressed logging camp cook named William Jamieson, who used to sit and play his fiddle for the passing steamships.

Although he enjoyed playing the instrument, his talent needed much practice. Bill Jamieson reputedly bought Fiddlers Bluff from Daniel Kells in 1867 for the sum of fifty dollars. Whitfield mentions that transaction in its records. The lonely man had no friends to speak of and would play his fiddle to pass the time. He took a land claim and built a shack near the Snohomish River, and those traveling by boat would hear the screech of his violin as they floated by. Sad and lonely, poor William finally decided to end his life and shot himself, committing suicide on the bluff. His only worldly possessions were a canoe and his violin. His neighbor Bobby Hughes took care of the burial for William and fashioned a grave marker with a very depressing epitaph carved on it: "Born in Misery, Lived in Misery, Died in Misery."

Supposedly, his violin and/or canoe were sold to pay for the poor man's burial. The grave marker was stuck into the ground near the Fiddler's grave. The actual grave site is unknown. Perhaps there is a house built on it? William Jamieson's actual date of death is conflicting.

Suicides produce the most tragic, trapped energy a death can create, as well as some of the angriest spirits. It is suggested by some that people who commit suicide often are unable to move to the next dimension and that their souls are trapped here, which is their punishment. Is the Fiddler's trapped soul still stuck on that hillside unable to move on?

In April 1888, the railroads—Seattle, Lakeshore and Eastern—completed a cut at Fiddlers Bluff that unearthed an ancient seabed. Countless fossilized clams, snails and other fossils were discovered. For almost one hundred years, hikers and amateur geologists carried away most of the specimens. People today still hike Fiddlers Bluff in the hopes of finding a rare fossil or two.

Locals still say that if the wind is still and the air is just so, one can hear the very faint, soft sound of the sad and lonely William playing his fiddle, although his music is still a little out of tune. A local historian noted, "The last steamboat through the river was the *Black Prince* in 1928. It was twenty-eight long with a crew of five men." He recalled, "The steamship that was carrying explosives for the blasting of Fiddlers Bluff area for the railroad was called *Nellie*, and they actually put themselves out of business because the creation of the railroad meant no more steamships were needed. The steamships would run from Woodinville through Fiddlers Bluff to Fall City."

KENWANDA GOLF COURSE ON FIDDLERS BLUFF

Kenwanda Golf Course is a local favorite and perhaps one that former owners have yet to leave. Ken and Wanda had dreams of creating a golf course on the slopes off Fiddlers Bluff near the Snohomish River. In 1963, they began planting trees and removing stones from the land with the help of friends and family. Finally, in 1967, they opened the back nine. The course has spectacular views of the town of Snohomish and the Cascade and Olympic Mountain Ranges, as well as the Snohomish River Valley. Ken and Wanda worked very hard to make their dream a reality. Today, the course is eighteen holes and includes 5,336 total yards. The name Kenwanda is derived from both of their names. Players, employees and neighbors whose homes back up the greens report seeing a lovely woman dancing on the back nine and believe that it is the spirit of Wanda. Unwilling to leave behind her beloved golf course they worked so hard to build, she continues to enjoy it whenever she feels like it. So, the next time you are teeing off and spot a beautiful lady out of the corner of your eye, it may be the spirit of Wanda wishing you a great game.

THE MALTBY CEMETERY, THE SNOHOMISH PIONEER CEMETERY AND GAR CEMETERY

THE MALTBY CEMETERY

The small Maltby Cemetery has established a reputation for being one of the most haunted sites in the state of Washington. For decades, ghost hunters have stumbled through the grounds, taking pictures and conducting séances and rituals in an effort to stir up the spirits there. It is said that if one descends the "13 Steps to Hell," by the time you get down to the last one, you lose your mind and go insane. Possibly they actually just led to a below-grade tomb for a wealthy family? Graveyard logic doesn't stop numerous frightening tales of people walking down the steps, only to get halfway and start screaming—the people return but can never talk again, and there are stories of people only getting a few steps down and becoming so uncomfortable that they try to rush back up; they feel the uncanny hand of someone trying to grab them and hold them there.

Unfortunately, the historic steps have long been destroyed. The rumor is that they were bulldozed in the 1990s to keep people away, and another rumor suggests that the police covered them up with a big concrete slab to discourage people from going to the cemetery because they were tired of the calls. Some of the gravestones and the grounds have been vandalized by inconsiderate ghost "hunters." The exact location of the cemetery is hard to find, as road markers have been removed to discourage visitors. (Note: The private property is off limits, and anyone found walking around on it will be prosecuted for trespassing. In order to visit it, you must have proof that you have a relative buried there, but the handful of people buried there are mostly descendants of the Doolittle family and can now rest in peace, and so can the groundskeeper. Unfortunately, overeager ghost hunters and non-respecting trespassers and vandals have ruined the experience for the rest of the people wanting to visit the Maltby Cemetery.)

Here is a story from Angela from Clearview:

> *When I was in high school, someone had tried to dig up one of the graves. All the tombstones were tipped over when we visited. It was sad. We all told each other ghost stories. The hike from the parking area to the cemetery was really creepy and definitely scared me to death. I just remember a lot of people used to go there and party. Lots of witch stories. I remember the steps; there was an upper part and a lower part. The first row of tombstones were tipped over. We tried to lift the tombstones back up to put them in place, but they were too heavy. There was a young child buried there, and that scared us. I swear at one point I could hear a baby cry. You never wanted to be there by yourself; it was too scary. It was about a ten-minute walk through the woods to get there, and there were stick crosses up through the trail in the woods…And this was* before *the* Blair Witch Project*! I always wondered what those little stick piles were, and then when I saw that movie, I really got creeped out. I never returned to the cemetery.*

Reports have also been made about large, full-bodied apparitions caught with both the naked eye and camera; loud noises and grunts coming from the bushes and heavily treed areas; a dreadful, creepy feeling coming over anyone entering the grounds; and a change in the air after you walk through the two pillars at the entrance. One of the larger gravestones is said to have "Order of Pendo" (supposedly a secret society) engraved at the bottom of it. Upon investigation, it seems there was some sort of organized society with that name out of California around 1897. It was a fraternal organization that was established sometime in 1894.

In 1882, Snohomish had three documented secret societies. Lodges and orders were generally a big part of social life in town. The first society was called the Masons, with several recognizable Snohomish names on the register like William Whitfield, E.C. Ferguson, Swett, Jackson and Folsom. The second order was called TMT, or the Mysterious Thirteen. The third was Forest Lodge No. 49, and Ferguson was also part of that group. Later, a fourth group called Knights of Labor came to Snohomish, forty-seven members strong. The local Snohomish Lodge was known as the Western Star and then later the Snohomish Lodge, No. 32, Knights of Pythias. Another group, Morton Post, No. 10, Grand Army of the Republic, was organized in 1884. Many more orders and groups were formed over the years.

Was there another local secret society called Order of Pendo? A branch of the California group? That might be just jumping to conclusions. Locals say that Order of Pendo was just a group of settlers who helped one another out in hard times.

While making the trek to the Maltby Cemetery, several abandoned automobiles can be found off the side of the cliff—the scrap metal remains of bad auto accidents? There have been legends of people being forced off the road when they try to visit the Maltby Cemetery by a big, black car and a phantom driver.

Here's a Maltby Cemetery story from a local resident:

> When I was little, my dad used to visit this cemetery. I don't remember who he was visiting or why he took me. I just remember how creepy it was. I would hold his hand as we walked through the trails that led to the tiny cemetery. I would never talk when there because I was scared the ghosts would hear me and come get us.

Multiple people report of their cars not starting after they return to them from a visit to the cemetery. No lights have been left on to drain the batteries. With so many reports of this phenomenon, it might be easy to conclude that a restless, angry spirit from an automobile wreck might be toying with the energy of the vehicle.

Other rumors concern a "Lady in Blue" and a small boy who have been seen walking down Paradise Lake Road. There are a lot of traffic accidents on Paradise Lake Road (even more now that it is common to text and drive), and possibly the Lady in Blue and the boy were a woman and her child who were unfortunately killed on the road. Walkers and joggers report serious "cold spots" on parts of the road even when the weather is hot.

Here is a story from Heidi:

> The scary stories about Maltby Cemetery are crazy! Rumors of demonic symbols, Freemasons, images of faces in photographs, obnoxious odors, voices caught on tape, extreme fog out of nowhere and more are a little frightening. Although I don't think you can go there anymore, I have been told stories in the past about witches, evil spirits, dark entities and more. I don't think I would visit there even if I could!

Here is a story from a neighbor:

> *I live near the Maltby Cemetery. I am too scared to visit it anymore because of all the stories. Plus I don't think you can go there anymore due to people vandalizing it. Sad. I think ghosts are real. People fail to realize that this world just might have more than just tales and stories. I love learning about our haunted history because it's nice to know that there might be life after death.*

THE PIONEER CEMETERY AND THE KIKENDALL CABIN

The Kikendall Cabin Historical Society website wrote about the history of the family and the cabin that is now located behind the modern-day Collector's Choice Restaurant (the "CCR"):

> *Kikendall built the Kikendall log cabin in 1875 on a 120 acre Pilchuck River homestead that was purchased for $1.50 an acre. The log cabin was located first north of Snohomish between the Snohomish-Machias Road, on the banks of the Pilchuck River. This cabin was once one of the pioneer landmarks of the area with its big stone fireplace, huge chinked logs and spacious porches. The first floor of the original cabin was just one room and extended to the back wall of the parlor. The cabin was twenty feet wide and sixteen feet deep. The Kikendall family moved into their new home in October of 1875. The kitchen area was added on the back about twenty years later (about 1895) increasing the depth to twenty-five feet. The second floor was used for sleeping quarters. When the cabin was eventually wired for electricity, the light bulb was located over the organ not only for light but to help keep the organ warm and dry during the winter months.*

Although no ghost stories have been discovered about the Kikendall Cabin, it is a wonderful little slice of time. Although not open to the public, the cabin is a great example of how the pioneers would build their homes in the late 1800s. The windows were boarded up to prevent vandalism to the Kikendall Cabin, but residents have been respectful of its history and try hard to preserve it.

Recently, a few amateur ghost hunters reported a sighting while investigating the Pioneer Cemetery, located on the outskirts of town. They

This page: The Pioneer Cemetery at one time had more than five hundred pioneers and Native Americans laid to rest. The making of the highway caused friction, as many bodies had to be moved to another location. A section of it is located next to the beautiful and historic Kikendall Cabin. *Author's collection.*

were walking carefully between the tombstones when, in the pitch black of night, they were suddenly surrounded by a glowing white mist about twenty feet in diameter. It swirled slowly around them for only a few short seconds and then vaporized—completely disappeared! They claimed that it seemed like it was just sucked up into the sky, and then there was total darkness again. Stunned and dumbfounded, there was no way to explain it.

It was reported in the *Seattle Times* in 2001, "Mary Low Sinclair, the eldest daughter of John and Lydia, established the Snohomish Cemetery. As a memorial to her late husband, a Snohomish pioneer, she deeded 3 acres for the town's first graveyard, which was christened in 1877. In 1902, the Snohomish Cemetery Association, the graveyard's custodian, declared no more burials would take place except for those already owning lots. The last burial was in 1923." One can view the remaining grave markers and pay respects to those spirits there.

Hauntings in cemeteries have been around as long as cemeteries have. For hundreds of years, people have visited cemeteries in the hopes of seeing a ghost or apparition. Braving the cold and damp midnight sky, ghost hunters toting cameras try to conjure up spirits in the hopes of capturing an image in film. It is said that at one time several hundred pioneers and Indians were buried at the old Pioneer Cemetery. Other bodies have been relocated to GAR Cemetery just outside the city of Snohomish.

Clara Blanche Gillespie (1878–1897)

Clara Gillespie died in 1897 while on her way to pick up her wedding dress during a fatal horse buggy accident. *Author's collection.*

A young, beautiful bride-to-be in search of her wedding gown should be a joyous event, but unfortunately for Ms. Gillespie, her day turned out to be the last day of her life. The Gillespie family moved to the Monroe area from Antrim, Michigan. Their daughter, Clara, soon fell in love with a lad named Mr. Braaten, and they had plans to get married.

One fateful day, in a horse and buggy borrowed from the girl's father, the young couple traveled from Monroe through Snohomish and then planned to move onward to Everett to purchase

This page: Horse-drawn carriages were a very common form of transportation for many people, but horses can be unpredictable and dangerous even when well trained. *Bill Betten.*

a wedding gown. They were to be married that June. As they passed through Snohomish toward Everett, they chose to stop and let their horse rest and get a drink of water. The bits in the animal's mouth complicated things, so Clara suggested taking the bridle off the horse in order for it to drink easier. Mr. Braaten removed the bridle, but the horse became startled. With no way to control the frightened animal, Mr. Braaten was dragged behind the horse, and poor Clara was thrown from the buggy onto the wooden plank road.

When Mr. Braaten was able to get up and return to his fiancée, he found her unconscious. She was taken to the nearest house, but Clara did not survive. Sadly, Mr. Braaten and Clara Gillespie never became man and wife. It wasn't too long after Clara's death that her father also had to bury his wife in the old cemetery, too. After an illness, Clara's mother succumbed on June 11, 1897. Some say that it was from a broken heart caused by the loss of her daughter. Some locals confess that traveling through the marsh area heading east out of town toward Everett, they spot a young girl wearing white walking through the fields. Could this be the restless spirit of young Clara, wearing her wedding gown after all and longing for the company of her groom? Her tombstone can be found today behind the Collector's Choice Restaurant west of the Kikendall Cabin in the old Pioneer Cemetery. Some people who have taken photographs of Clara's tombstone report a shiny, glowing light emanating from behind the stone. Others report a cold chill when they walk by—simply the wind or the spirit of young, agitated Clara, who never got to enjoy her wedding day?

GAR Cemetery

The beautiful and expansive GAR Cemetery (Grand Army of the Republic) is said to be the final resting place of many prominent local pioneers, such as John and Lydia Low, Pilchuck Julie (the "Indian princess of Snohomish") and individuals from the families Bailey, Dubuque, Ludwig, Stocker, Blackman, Cathcart, Maughlin and Bakeman, as well as many others. The expansive GAR is owned and operated by the Earl Winehart Post No. 96, the American Legion building in town. GAR is a Civil War cemetery that was established in 1898 and opened in 1901 by Morton Post No. 110 of Snohomish; about two hundred Union veterans are buried there. It is one of the only two Civil War GAR cemeteries in the state of Washington. In the northwest corner of the grounds is a fantastic GAR monument that was dedicated in 1914 and represents the "cavalry, navy and artillery surrounding and supporting a southern-facing, full-sized, uniformed and armed infantry sentry, alertly standing guard over his sleeping comrades in arms." More than four thousand people came from all over the country to attend the dedication of the memorial.

A March 20, 2016 article from the *Sky Valley Chronicle* reads:

> *There are as many as 16,000 people buried in the state of Washington who survived the horrible Civil War that later moved, lived and died in the Pacific Northwest. There may be over 700 veterans of the war buried in Snohomish County alone. Washington was not yet a state when the Civil War began but it turns out that Isaac Stevens, our state's (then only a territory) Governor was killed carrying the Union flag in 1862 during the Battle of Chantilly. Stevens was the territory's Governor from 1853–1857.*

Here is a ghost story from Carol:

> *My Grandmother was what I would call psychic, and one of the most interesting stories I can recall growing up was when the son of one of her friends died due to the war. She was in the kitchen cooking up a storm like always, and all of a sudden she stopped moving and looked at the wall. She had an odd look on her face. It bothered me very much. I later discovered that she had a strange feeling come over her, and she knew right away someone had passed over. In her kitchen that day, she had seen this boy's boots. Apparently, he had a pair of favorite boots that my grandma recognized. Sure enough, Grandma had gotten a phone call a few days later letting her know that he had been killed. I am not sure why the apparition of his boots revealed themselves in my grandma's kitchen that day, but maybe it was his way of getting her attention. She was able to comfort her friend better knowing his spirit lived on.*

The Civil War was a bloody battle that began in 1861 and lasted four years. It was estimated that about 620,000 soldiers died in those few years, most only twenty-five years old. New studies by Dr. J. David Hacker have determined that the number of casualties may be much higher, as many as 850,000. Through army documents, pension and census records, he discovered that the original number of deaths was inaccurate. As for the horses that served in the Civil War, it is estimated that 1.5 million, possibly even as high as 3.5 million, lost their lives to the cause. For each soldier lost, five horses gave their lives.

Most soldiers were buried right where they lost their lives, for there often wasn't time to stop and have proper burials. Later, many bodies were exhumed and moved to proper cemeteries, but it is thought that tens of thousands of men are resting in unmarked graves, possibly covered now by parking lots and shopping malls.

The Northern states had an army of 22 million strong, whereas the Southern states had an army of just 9 million men. Soldiers earned just thirteen dollars per month, and if you were a black man, you earned only seven dollars per month to fight the war.

With seven hundred veterans buried in the county, it is no wonder people have had sightings of soldiers at GAR Cemetery in Snohomish. Washington is honored to provide two of the GAR Civil War cemeteries in its state.

Snohomish County did not get forgotten during World War I, and these brave men should not go unnoticed. Boys volunteered from Snohomish, Lake Stevens, Monroe, Bothell, Duvall, Machias and Arlington to become part of two coast artillery companies: the Twelfth and the Fifth. At 5:30 a.m. on August 1, 1917, the young men were to start their journey from Everett and Snohomish onward to war. It is estimated that about three thousand men left the county for their frightening future. The war lasted from 1914 to 1918 and involved thirty countries. It took the lives of 9 million men, and another 21 million were wounded. At the Battle of the Somme in France, thirty thousand died in one day. It was a tragic loss, as with any war. Many of these men were just eighteen years old at the time of their death. Although they did not die in Snohomish, it would be nice to think that their spirits came back home to be with their family and loved ones.

The Snohomish GAR Cemetery is also the final resting place for a very unique, bonded, lifelong couple. O.B. Allen died in 1902, and his final wish was for his body to be embalmed and kept in a vault until the love of his life could join him in eternal peace. His wife finally passed away in 1908, and his wish was granted. While alive, Allen was a local blacksmith and police officer, as reported in the 1908 *Everett Daily Herald*.

The second GAR Cemetery location is in Seattle at 1200 East Howe Street. That one was established in 1895 and is nestled up on Capitol

Hill, next to the Lakeview Cemetery. It is maintained by the City of Seattle. The cemetery has more than five hundred gravesites and is more than one hundred years old. Nearby, neighbors have reported hearing screams late at night, ghostly apparitions of soldiers dressed ready for battle and even a beautiful phantom war horse running through the graves and jumping the tombstones.

The Railroad and Lumber Mill Tragedies

The Railroad

It is hard to imagine life in Snohomish before 1860, when there were fewer than fifty white men living in the county. The land was not yet surveyed or marked; there were no towns, stores, roads, churches or schools built yet. In 1861, the formation of the county was developed. Written documents were finally being stored, and things were becoming recorded, such as the first sale: "one yoke of stags, seven years old," sold for $1.50. One of the first recorded land claims was a transfer from "P. Odien to W.B. Sinclair for $455."

In 1883, before the arrival of the railroads, the means of transportation were very limited to canoes, horses and by foot. In the late 1870s, there were maybe three wagons in the whole county; soon, many were fortunate enough to have wagons on their farms. This was also the year Snohomish decided that it needed a road to Seattle. Work on the wagon road began south of Lake Washington, and the following year, work started at Snohomish. It is written that with the hard work of just twenty or so volunteers, the task of creating a road and getting to Seattle and back was becoming a reality that would take just a single day—versus the steamship route of two days' travel time. Seattle in the late 1800s was not much bigger than Snohomish, and it did not offer better facilities or luxuries, but trade was still a necessity for locals.

Today, when thousands of people drive the route of Highway 9 to 522 to I-5 South to get from Snohomish to Seattle twenty-nine miles south, it is

Life in 1865 was pretty rough, and the Blue Eagle Saloon was a common watering hole for locals. It was built where the bottom of Cedar Street is now located. *Snohomish Historical Society, FS-025, originally by photographer Sammis from New York.*

almost unimaginable to think that just a few dozen men could even create such a road. In 1884, the sum of $150 was needed to make the road "fit for a wagon"—today, a very small improvement on the same highway costs more like $150 million!

The first real train running from Seattle to Snohomish began on July 3, 1888, although it had to stop on the south side of the Snohomish River because there was no bridge constructed at that time. It carried a whopping twelve passengers, but it left Snohomish with forty eager travelers, all making the historic first train trip to Seattle. The bridge was completed in 1888, and the first train rolled across it on September 15, 1888. The townsfolk were thrilled.

But the rejoicing would be short-lived, as the mighty Snohomish River had other plans once again. That year in October, it decided to flood the small town, wrecking everything in its path. The bridge quickly became jammed with 700,000 feet of logs, and then the boom broke on the Pilchuck River, forcing another 3 million feet of logs toward the Snohomish River bridge. The bridge was doomed.

Above: A Snohomish Dye Works horse carriage, taking a break on the southeast corner of Union and Second Street in downtown Snohomish. *Snohomish Historical Society, BU-071.*

Right: The Telegraph and Post Office Building was located at 119 Union. *Snohomish Historical Society, BU-094a.*

Three men pose in front of the Telegraph and Post Office Building. Snohomish Dye Works was behind the post office. *Snohomish Historical Society, BU-095.*

Inside the post office, workers pose for the camera on July 9, 1907. The Postal Telegraph Company came to Snohomish County in 1886. In October 1883, Postmaster Wilbur sold 160 money orders totaling $3,798.42 in one month. *Snohomish Historical Society, BU-063.*

It is noted that in 1893, the Great Northern Railroad was offering the ride to and from Marysville to Snohomish. The fare was seventy cents and took one hour and twenty minutes, the quickest ride ever made at that time. Today, the trip from Snohomish to Marysville is fifteen miles and takes just twenty minutes.

On January 28, 1889, the mail finally came via train to Snohomish for the very first time. Also in 1889, the area known as south Snohomish was platted, with the lots selling for $100 to $175. Railroad improvements for 1889 totaled $150,000, with part of that utilized for repair of the railroad bridge that had been damaged during the last flood.

Railroad and lumber mill deaths plague almost any frontier town, and Snohomish is no exception. Dozens of accidental deaths of engineers and workers were reported in local newspapers such as the *Everett Herald* and the *Snohomish County Tribune*. Workers risked their lives daily, and as reported in an advertisement for help by Northern Pacific Railroad Company in the *Snohomish County Tribune* in 1922, wages were detailed as, "Boilermakers .70 cents per hour, Freight Car Men .63 cents per hour and Helpers All Class .47 cents per hour."

Many lives have been taken on the railroad tracks, one unfortunately being that of Indian chief Pilchuck Jack, the last chief of the Pilchuck Indian

The Snohomish River, with the Bruhn and Henry and Henry Scharf Wharf and Storage Building, as well as the steamship *Skagit Queen*, circa 1906. *Snohomish Historical Society, FS-017.*

tribe and husband to Indian "princess" Julie Pilchuck. He died tragically one night as he was struck by a moving train while walking along the train tracks from south Snohomish to Cathcart in November 1905. Jack was known by locals as the "King of the Pilchucks," a small tribe who often fished in the river for salmon. The word *Pilchuck* takes its name from the Chinook Indian jargon words *pill*, meaning red, and *chuck*, meaning water. Pilchuck Jack was well respected and liked in the community, and when he passed, the town honored him with a beautiful funeral procession and parade through town.

Princess Julia Pilchuck died of smallpox in April 1923, as did many of the local Indians, who could not tolerate the diseases brought here by the "white men." Unfortunately, their tribes almost went extinct by the year 1900. Contagious diseases common during these times included smallpox, scarlet fever and, the most horrifying, black diphtheria, which killed many people for several years; in 1877, its dreaded arrival came to Snohomish. The bacteria would kill most of the children it struck. Even as late as 1921, the United States recorded 206,000 cases of diphtheria and 15,520 deaths. Before there was treatment for diphtheria, up to half of the people who got the disease died from it. It was spread from an infected person by a cough or a sneeze. It can also be spread through common contact, such as sharing a toy or bike. Obviously, it was a dreadful fate for the citizens of Snohomish to have the disease in their town threatening their lives. A thin, gray layer of bacteria would coat the infected person's throat and lungs. Tracheotomies were performed at that time for relief, but the survival rate for the procedure, compounded by the complications from the disease, was extremely low. Local newspapers listed many sad deaths of Snohomish children who had succumbed to the dreadful ailment at early ages.

It quickly spread through the county, and in 1878, it took the entire Howe family, with five children, within just a few weeks. A few months later, it took unfortunate hold of Ferguson's daughter, Ethel. Snohomish was not safe from the horrific diseases that plagued the times.

The first doctor in the county was Dr. H. Smith, and he lived near the mouth of the Snohomish River but then moved to Seattle. The next doctor for the town was Dr. E.C. Folsom, a graduate from Harvard, who arrived in the fall of 1872. During the dreaded diphtheria period, Dr. Folsom bravely and untiringly treated his patients inflicted with the terrifying disease. Dr. Folsom spent thirteen years practicing medicine in the little town of Snohomish. The beloved Dr. Folsom became fatally ill and died at age fifty-nine on May 15, 1885. In 1887, the town erected a monument made from Italian marble in his honor, now located at the GAR Cemetery in town. The great doctor was first buried along Pilchuck Creek, and later his body was moved to GAR Cemetery.

Before smallpox took her life, Princess Julia Pilchuck was most famous for her interesting snowfall prediction one year. The snow in town started in January 1916 and continued through February, causing much havoc and frustration with the locals. The little town got hammered with more than forty-two inches of snow, and some worried that roofs would collapse under the weight. Frozen water can cause many troubles now, let alone in the early 1900s, when plumbing was a nightmare.

Julia somehow predicted a snowstorm that would be "two squaws deep." Newspaper articles ran her prediction in 1917, one year later. Both years had extreme snowfall, with 1916 being the worst of the two. The *Edmonds Tribune-Review* reported, "Last Saturday evening the betting odds against Pilchuck Julia prophecy of snow this winter being 'two squaws deep' was at least 100 to one against the prophetess, but presto, Sunday morning people in the Sound began to realize that they were in the grip of a blizzard and Pilchuck Julia's stock began to climb."

One has to wonder: if Princess Julia could predict the weather, she most certainly could come back to haunt her old stomping grounds. Julia was buried in the old Indian cemetery and was moved to GAR in 1947, when the new Stevens Pass Highway was built. Jack and Julia Pilchuck have a memorial shaft at the GAR Cemetery in Snohomish. Although no one knows the accurate ages of Jack and Julia, it is said that she lived to be about one hundred years old.

Homeowners today who live in houses near the railroad tracks report strange and unusual lights, train whistle horns blowing that don't sound quite like the horns installed in the engines today and ghostly figures walking down the middle of the tracks at all hours of the night. The unnerving yapping and high-pitched cries from wild coyotes down by the tracks make risky, late-night walks by locals even scarier.

Many deaths have occurred while walking the train tracks in Snohomish. An early pioneer named William Romines, who came to Snohomish in 1872 with the hopes and dreams of being a hotel proprietor, was tragically killed one day on the tracks. Before his death, he purchased the Riverside Hotel that was on Maple Street from John Low for $1,500. In 1877, Romines then purchased the wharf near his hotel and sold logging supplies but sold that within months. Romines placed this ad in the *Northern Star* newspaper dated January 22, 1876: "All persons that have claims against me are requested to present the same for settlement on or before the 1st

The railroad was an important part of Snohomish's history and development but also the cause of a lot of tragic casualties and deaths. *Author's collection.*

of February 1876. All persons indebted to me MUST settle by the 1st of February in order to save costs. I am going out of business and must have all my affairs settled. William Romines."

In 1892, he moved to a little town east of Snohomish called Skykomish and soon became a "county charge," a person who needs help from the county due to mental or physical problems. But locals found William friendly, and he soon earned the nickname "Uncle Billy." He died on the railroad tracks while walking from the county farm to Snohomish.

The death toll from railroad accidents mounts as one reads through the old newspapers. As reported in the *Monroe Monitor* on October 26, 1906 ("Wreck Sunday Morning"): "Trains collide on the Great Northern Railway at Fern Bluff near Monroe on October 21, 1906. A Skykomish local passenger train due into Monroe at 7:35 a.m. crashes into an eastbound freight train at Fern Bluff, two and a half miles east of Monroe. Both trains are traveling at full speed. Both locomotives were demolished. Two firemen and an engineer aboard the smaller train were killed and several passengers were injured." The *Snohomish County Tribune* reported on

June 5, 1895, "Brakeman Keener took a misstep and fell before a moving train killing him instantly." And again, on January 26, 1900, the *Snohomish County Tribune* reported that a "35 year old man named Kingsley, a logger of Smith & Miniger, was struck by a train after he fell asleep near the tracks." Another was reported in the *Everett Daily Herald* on September 15, 1902, as "A.C. Alexander of Oleson's Logging was struck by a train and not expected to make it until the morning hours."

Report after report can be read of persons and workers being injured or killed by railroad cars. Even as safe as the railroads have become, there are still deaths and tragedies due to accidents on the rail roads. One man named Lyle, who lives past Fiddlers Bluff, announced, "They hardly ever run a train on the tracks by my old house, but I can hear the faint blow of an unknown whistle and the creaky, metal scraping sound of the trains near my place late at night. Sometimes I get up and look out my window hoping to see an actual train so I can tell myself I am not losing my mind, but there is no train running."

THE LUMBER MILLS AND LOGGING CAMPS

Logging was the staple of early businesses in Snohomish. Once the train came to Snohomish regularly in 1881, the town boomed. There was a great demand for lumber for both railroad construction and buildings, and Snohomish had a grand selection of tall, straight fir trees just waiting to be logged. Some of the trees had one thousand rings to their life—a shame to cut them down.

In 1887, Snohomish spent $45,000 to improve the look of the city, and the following year, real estate exploded. In one month, real estate sales exceeded $30,000, and the population of Snohomish doubled to about 2,500 people.

During the period of the 1860s and 1870s, there were about twenty logging camps with 237 hardworking men and 234 strong oxen for pulling. In 1864, it was estimated that an incredible 350 million feet of logs were cut and hauled just in Snohomish County. The town offered the excellent combination for logging—countless timbers of great strength and a nearby river to carry the lumber away.

The Blackman brothers started a lumber mill in 1883 near where the Ironworks location and visitors' center are today. They soon began churning out red cedar shingles. The Blackman brothers moved from

In 1892, tall, strong trees were a big draw for settlers, not only as a means of making money but also as material for constructing homes and buildings. *David Dilgard, Everett Public Library, Northwest Room.*

An early pioneer proudly stands before his cabin in 1892. Hundreds of timbers tower in the background. *David Dilgard, Everett Public Library, Northwest Room.*

Maine to Washington in 1872 and found their homes in Snohomish in 1875. They ran the lumber mills in town from 1875 through 1907 and then became interested in the Wenatchee area, although they remained a very big part of Snohomish. In 1911, the Cascade Mill in town employed one hundred men.

Arthur Blackman opened a grocery store in town in 1883 that is now the Oxford Saloon at 913 First Street. It had a hitching post for horses out front and looked very much like it does today. During Prohibition, the Oxford Saloon was called the Oxford Pool Room, as it didn't serve liquor until World War II.

In November 1910, the nearby town of Everett voted to become a "dry" town, so liquor would no longer be served. That shut down dozens and dozens of area bars. Prohibition was seen as a way to protect "malnourished children and neglected wives," as it would keep the breadwinner's money in his pocket for his family instead of finding its way into the local bar's cash register. Since Snohomish was not a dry town, the thirsty citizens of Everett flocked to Snohomish to party and drink. The words *bootleggers*, *scofflaws* and *rumrunners* became household terms. Local loggers got the rap for notoriously

In the 1950s, the Oxford Saloon is on the right, with Neil Electric (Beck's Antiques), Noble Tavern (Time Out Tavern) and Stage Depot. Looking east is Tradewell (Union Bakery). *Snohomish Historical Society, FS-023.*

During Prohibition, the nearby Everett was a "dry" town, so many citizens would make the trek to Snohomish to wet their whistles and enjoy the atmosphere of the local pubs and restaurants. *Bill Betten.*

blowing their paychecks on booze, gambling and ladies. They figured that they worked hard, so they could afford to play hard. And they did.

With Everett being a dry town, even after the big fire of 1911, it is rumored that the saloons in Snohomish didn't even wait for the embers to cool down before the bars opened back up, ready to serve booze.

In 1890, a Seattle investor named J.A. Panting from a company called Huron Lumber moved to Snohomish. He invested $25,000 in the city, which included the Noll Shingle Mill. At the same time, seven hundred lots were sold in one week, creating the new Panting Addition, at the price of $10 to $15 per lot. Just two years later, an isolated house in the Painting Addition bought by the council and used as a pest house was burned to the ground to satisfy nervous neighbors.

The Snohomish Land Company was organized by the ever-eager E.C. Ferguson, H.C. Pettit and G.G. England, and they promptly solicited forty thousand pamphlets advertising new lots for sale in town.

Logging is still one of the most dangerous jobs out there. Even with all of today's technology, accidents still happen that claim lives. One of the very real but unfortunate and unfair facts about the logging and railroad

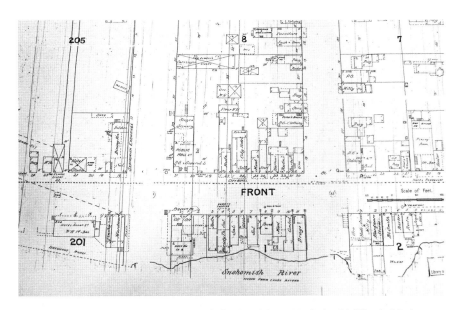

A hand-drawn map of Downtown Historic Snohomish, 1890. *Snohomish Historical Society, photo from author's collection.*

community back then was that these accidents were sometimes swept under the rug or minimized.

Logging accidents were common and sadly affected many families. Many newspaper articles and obituaries can be found in regards to the danger of logging and shingle making. One example is from the *Labor Journal*, dated January 7, 1909: "Curtis Blacker was instantly killed just before quitting time Monday night at Williams Company Logging just 5 miles from Snohomish, by being struck by a log. He was in charge of a crew of men swamping out a skid road and gave the signal for the donkey engine to start. Just as he did so, a fellow workman yelled out, 'Look out!' He replied, 'Oh, I'm all right— go ahead.' Unfortunately, the engine started and the log rolled over, killing him." When one looks at homes and buildings that were built under such dangerous and compromising conditions back then, it is sad to think of the sacrifices and losses families endured in order to construct them. Many men were killed while working the mills and logging, and if the operations were still around today, I am sure that there would be plenty of angry and restless spirits haunting them.

As important as these workers were to the town and community, they were considered "lower level" citizens by some. The men would come into town looking for fun and enjoy spending their money on gambling, whiskey

The arrival of the Great Northern Railroad in 1893 set the stage for a huge wave of logging activity that supported many local families and businesses. Logging and sawmills soon became the largest industry and continued until the end of World War II. *Library of Congress.*

and women. Many brawls, stabbings and arguments arose from the group of rowdy men with a little too much to drink. When crime in town would become too much, concerned citizens would complain to the authorities, but not much would be done except an occasional "clean up campaign." During late-night walks on First Street, it would be fun to spot a ghost or two from one of these mischief-making spirits.

Logging mills and camps were a familiar sight in early Snohomish and provided a lot work for locals. One of the most influential families in the lumber business was the Blackman family, originally from Maine. The three brothers moved to the Northwest in 1872. Their mill provided many jobs for locals, and the three brothers also built many buildings in town.

Smallpox often ran rampant through the railroad camps and mills. For an unvaccinated person, the chance of dying was almost 50 percent. Millions of people died throughout the world of the dreaded smallpox during the 1800s. An English doctor noted that milkmaids did not get the fateful smallpox disease but instead the less serious version called cowpox. Thus the connection was made: getting smallpox meant you were less likely to develop and die from smallpox.

Snohomish residents were not free from the scare and effects of the deadly disease. Seattle and Everett would not allow Snohomish residents to enter their towns for fear of contracting the disease. This isolation continued for almost a year. In 1890, the population of Snohomish was about two thousand people.

In 1892, the town suffered a great smallpox curse, with the first person affected in town being F.H. Hoskinson in June. From that point forward, there was one new case of smallpox reported every week. Tragically, eleven people died in town from the disease. Some locals felt that this had been introduced by the railroad camps. The plague advanced so quickly in a victim's body that many were at death's door before they even knew they were affected. Such a panic ensued that schools closed, churches suffered, meetings were held off and people generally stayed inside the protection of their homes. The City of Seattle made threats of quarantine from Snohomish and King County and stalled all trains coming from Snohomish until it felt that the disease was under control. Steamships were also ordered to stop their routes to Snohomish. Everett soon jumped aboard the smallpox quarantine craze and ordered Snohomish residents to stay out of its city, too. In 1893, Everett would report having twenty-one cases of smallpox.

THE SNOHOMISH RIVER

The Snohomish River has always been a blessing and a curse to those living near it. Before automobiles and railroads, the river was the best form of transportation. If the river was shut down, as in the case of it freezing over so boats were unable to use it, hardships would be felt. Most supplies, lumber and food were brought by boat. The Snohomish River is notorious for flooding, and during these episodes, it has killed thousands of head of livestock.

The first boats (and form of transportation other than horses) in Snohomish were, of course, Native American log canoes. These were carefully crafted by the same men who also carved the totems with such great care and skill. Some of these log canoes could hold up to fifty men. The craft was a skill passed on from father to son and represented a very high and respected position within the tribe.

Chief Patkanim ruled the Snohomish tribe as well as the Snoqualmie one. He was a friendly but strong chief, and it is rumored that he protected the white people from hostile Indians. In an article written in 1885 by Bagley and posted in the *Seattle Post-Intelligencer*, supposedly, in a show of good faith toward the whites, Chief Patkanim killed two men by hanging them and then chopped off their heads. The heads were then sent to the white men as "a guaranty of good faith." In another article, it is reported that Patkanim fought for ten hours with another group, a battle that ended in nine deaths. Apparently, one did not mess with Chief Patkanim. When the chief died, a memorial was erected in Everett at the intersection of Wetmore and

Traveling via the Snohomish River was an excellent way to get around before automobiles. *Snohomish Historical Society, BU-089.*

California in 1922. There are probably many more murders that occurred during this period, but records of such are hard to find.

The earliest boat that traveled the Snohomish River was a schooner called the *Gazelle* and was built in 1864 at Mukilteo. Many fine vessels were being built in Mukilteo during this period. Two of the most well-known boats that traveled the river during 1876 were called *Nellie* and the *Fanny Lake*.

The *Nellie* was a favorite in town, and almost everyone living in Snohomish had ridden on it at some time or another. As noted in the *Northern Star*, "Nellie was 80 feet in length and her first trip was to Snoqualmie Falls launched from Seattle on July 22, 1866." The first time *Nellie* came to Snohomish was in August. As reported in the *Northern Star* issue on September 2, 1876, "On her trial run from Olympia to Seattle, August 26, 1876, the Nellie made the sixty miles in four hours and forty minutes."

The deep, cold waters of the Snohomish River and surrounding waters have taken many lives over the years—Thomas MacIntosh in 1882, Dan O'Neil in 1885 and then, at the same spot, Jesse Dutcher in 1887.

In April 1882, the *Nellie* was purchased by Captain Charles Low, son of J.N. and Lydia Low, original pioneers in Snohomish. After he got the *Nellie* up and running, he bought another steamer in 1886 called the *Monroe* for $8,000 in order to compete with the rivaling ship the *Cascade*.

The Snohomish River and productive lumber mills, where countless shingles were produced to be shipped all over. *Snohomish Historical Society, FS-020.*

The very well-liked and successful Captain Low died suddenly on June 12, 1887, when a blood vessel exploded in his brain, killing him almost instantly. Legend tells of a Dr. D.J. Stansbury, a medium staying in Snohomish, who dictated a spirit message from the late Captain Low, for which the note and signature were exact matches of Low's very recognizable handwriting. The *Golden Gate* noted:

> *Dr. D.J. Stansbury, slate medium, once of San Francisco, is very successful in obtaining spiritual writing in public as well as in private. There came upon the slates at Dr. Stansbury's public séance, last Sunday evening, the following message from Judge Wm. R. Thompson, father of H.M. Thompson, of this city: "The essential principles of primitive Christianity and the precepts of Modern Spiritualism are essentially one and the same, which, if practiced, would lead to the highest standard of morality and be the means of grace by which all might be saved."*

Did Captain Low really send spiritual medium Stansbury a handwritten message from the other side? It would be wonderful to find a copy of it. Slate writing was popular back in those times, and a so-called medium would perform séances to speak to the dead. Two slates were pinned together, and the spirit would write a message on the boards in chalk. Some tried to prove that the act was fraudulent, while others tried to prove of its existence. Dr. Stansbury was a prominent medium in his time and actively practiced slate writing and other types of spiritual activities. Today, "automatic writing" is essentially the same thing, but the medium uses pens and paper instead of chalkboards.

The Snohomish River is notorious for flooding nearby homes, businesses, pastures and barns. In 1892, the mighty Snohomish River was twenty feet above low water and washed out all the bridges above Snohomish. A brave young girl named May Feak noticed that part of the train tracks was under water and quickly ran down the track to notify the conductor of the problem. She potentially saved the lives of two hundred people. She received a life pass from the Great Northern for her act.

It flooded again in 1921, 1951 and 1975, in the last damaging more than three hundred homes and killing 3,500 head of livestock, including a few horses. Dead cows could be seen piled up in places where the floodwater had finally gone down. Heavy rainfall in 1986 brought another bout of flooding, and then once more in 1990, the rain coupled with the "Pineapple Express."

The Snohomish bridge in 1892. In January 1890, the bridge over the Pilchuck River was built under the direct supervision of John Iles and cost about $1,500. *David Dilgard, Everett Public Library, Northwest Room.*

Isaac Cathcart came to Snohomish County in 1869 to be a "laborer in the woods." In 1872, he built the Exchange Hotel and by 1890 owned five thousand acres; he became one of the richest men in the county. It has a great waterfront view from the Snohomish River. *Snohomish Historical Society, FS-018.*

The dike broke in more than ten spots, and the flooding began to take over the town once again. Men and more than one hundred cattle drowned.

Can animals come back as spirits? Many people claim to have seen their beloved pets return to their side in times of stress or sorrow, as if to comfort their old masters. Others swear that they have heard the meow of a deceased cat, the bark of a dog or even the whinny of a horse. Perhaps the grieving owner simply misses the pet so much that their mind is playing tricks on them. Or is it possible that animals can come back into this dimension to visit their owners?

Here is a haunting story from "TJ," now living in Marysville:

> *I used to live in Snohomish down by the train tracks and across from the Snohomish River. I sold just before the last bad flood, in 2006 I think it was. We had a couple horses on our property that the kids used to ride. I know a lot of animals got killed during floods when the river would rise so fast there wasn't even time to act, let alone save cattle and horses. I heard the horrible stories about all the farm animals that drowned in the floods here in town, and it really made me sad. The thing that sticks in my head happened some time before the last flood hit*

town again. I was looking out my back window at the horses, sick of all the rain we had been having lately, when I could have sworn I saw a cow in the pasture with my horses. At first I thought maybe a neighbor's cow got loose, as that happens now and then, but it was inside the pasture with my horses. I thought to myself, "Now how did that cow get in the pasture? I must have a broken fence…" so I pulled my boots on and grabbed a rain coat and headed out back to the horse pasture. When I got closer, I didn't see a cow anywhere. I thought it had just moved on, so I decided to check the fence before my horses got out into the road or something. I walked the whole perimeter of the fence, and not one area had a downed wire or broken board. I have no idea where the cow went or if I even really saw it. I soon moved my horses to my friend's house up on the hill. I always wondered if that cow was the spirit of one that had been killed in a previous flood and it was warning me of the upcoming one and that I needed to protect my animals. Sure enough, Snohomish flooded that year.

And here is a sad story by Dale of Marysville:

I cannot ever look at the river in Snohomish and not think of a sad story I was told as a teenager long ago. Supposedly, a young boy was fishing for salmon off the river some years back, near the bridge one evening. When he never came home, his family started to worry. When it became late into the night and he still wasn't home, they really began to worry. When the next morning came around and the boy still wasn't home, the parents started to panic and called the police. Now this was before the time of cellphones, keep in mind. A search party was called, and everyone looked for the boy for days. After a while, the search team dwindled, and the family resigned to the terrible fact that maybe their son would never return from fishing. Days turned into weeks, weeks turned into months and months turned into years. It wasn't until several decades later [that] another fisherman was down by the river and his line became snagged on something. It ended up being the boy's remains. Every single time I drive past that bridge, I think about that poor boy and his family and how he was down there the whole time until finally someone found him. I always say a little prayer for him now every time I go fishing.

CONCLUSION

Stories of ghosts, hauntings and restless spirits have been around as long as living people have been alive, and they will continue until the end of time. Perhaps people are fascinated by them because they want some sort of proof that there is life after death. They desire to know that their loved ones are not suffering or simply because they are interested.

As technology advances, the desire to capture proof of their existence has increased dramatically and is no longer limited to Ouija boards, crystal balls, tea leaves, psychics and slate writers. People do not frown upon those who choose to believe in ghosts and the spirit world as much as they did in the past. It is very common to hear conversations about ghosts and spirits almost everywhere you go.

Snohomish has tugged at people's hearts since its development, and people continue to love its century-old streets and charming historic buildings. As they roam in and out of the stores, I hope that they find these stories from the past fascinating, frightening and intriguing. I also hope this book makes them stop in the entryways of the Oxford Saloon, Fred's Tavern or any of the other wonderful stores or buildings in Snohomish and pause for just a second to remember those pioneers who worked so hard to create the wonderful, picturesque town that everyone loves today.

Old businesses here include Snohomish Hardware, Western Auto, Bowling, Brown's Theater, Oxford Saloon, Keaton's Sporting Goods, Trent's Café, Harmon's and the Chevrolet Building. *Snohomish Historical Society, FS-024.*

And who knows, maybe they will even spot a dark apparition lurking in a corner somewhere or hear the faint whispers of a restless Snohomish ghost asking for help. Or, hopefully, they might feel the lightest touch of a cold hand as it tries to caress the side of their face as they slowly turn to walk away...

SOURCES

Buchanan's Journal of Man, May 1887. Vol. 1, no. 4. Project Gutenberg. www. gutenberg.net.

Centers for Disease Control and Prevention. "About Diphtheria." http:// www.cdc.gov/diphtheria/about/index.html.

Civil War Trust. "Civil War Facts." http://www.civilwar.org/education/ history/faq.

Dubuque, Ruth Brodigan. "Fiddler—They Called His Bluff." *Everett Herald*, February 1929.

Everett Daily Herald. "Death of Engineer Riley and Kittle." May 8, 1902.

Everett Herald. September 29, 2001.

Fieldtripper app. fieldtripper.com.

Folsom, Dr. E.C. *History of Skagit and Snohomish Counties.* Chicago: published by Interstate Publishing Company, printed by S.J. Clarke Company, 1906. Includes his biographical sketch.

Grace, Oscar. "Pilchuck Julia's Predictions May Come to Pass." Editorial. *Tribune-Review*, February 2, 1917. Reprinted by Betty Lou Gaeng, 2010. www.snohomishwomenslegacy.org.

HistoryLink. "Prohibition in Washington State." historylink.org.

The History of Vaccines. "The History of Diptheria." http://www. historyofvaccines.org/content/timelines/diphtheria.

McMurchy, Catherine. "Grave Now Marked." *Seattle Examiner*, May 25, 2002.

Monroe Monitor. "Wreck Sunday Morning." October 26, 1906. Available at historylink.org.

Northern Star. "Early Settlers." January 22, 1876.

Oxford Saloon. "Haunted History." http://www.oxfordsaloonsnohomish. com/haunted-history.

Primary Facts. "World War I: Facts and Information." http://primaryfacts. com/1645/world-war-1-facts-and-information.

River Reflections. Vol 1. Snohomish, WA: Snohomish Historical Society, Snohomish Publishing Company, Inc., 1981. Miscellaneous Snohomish history. With original research by Dorothy Colquhoun; Ione Gale, 1946– 49; and Ruth and Stan Dubuque.

Sky Valley Chronicle. "Civil War Dead Honored at GAR Cemetery." March 20, 2016.

Snohomish Carnegie Library. http://www.snohomishcarnegie.org.

Snohomish Chamber of Commerce. "Historic Downtown Snohomish." www.cityofsnohomish.com.

Snohomish County Tribune. Advertisements, prices and building information, 1894–present. Newspaper archives, Snohomish Library, Snohomish, Washington.

———. "Death Robs a Bridegroom." April 1897.

———. Miscellaneous Blackman family info. April 14, 1927.

———. Various articles, 1910–45.

———. "Wroth Murder." November 1, 1895. Also published on Monday, August 3, 2009, at herald.net.

Snohomish County website. http://snohomishcountywa.gov.

Snohomish Eye. Advertisements, prices and building information, 1882–97. Newspaper archives, Snohomish Library, Snohomish, Washington.

———. Various articles, 1882–97.

Time Life Books. *Hauntings.* N.p.: self-published, 1989.

Wells, Russ, and Sandy Wells, of the Paranormal Research and Investigation team, with owner Sondra McCutchan. Information on the Cabbage Patch Restaurant, gathered in 2007.

Whitfield, William. *History of Snohomish County, Washington.* Vol. 1. Chicago: Pioneer Historical Publishing Company, 1926.

Wierdus.com. Oxford article.

Wikipedia. "Snohomish, Washington." https://en.wikipedia.org/wiki/Snohomish,_Washington.

About the Author

Deborah Cuyle currently lives in Snohomish and loves everything about the small town. She has written two other travel books: *Cannon Beach, Oregon: Images of America* and *Kidding Around Portland*. Her passions include local history, animals, the beach, art and writing. Her historic Snohomish farm is home to multiple rescued animals, including a three-legged cat, and she also provides a horsemanship program to Girl Scouts. She enjoys thinking about the possibility of an afterlife and especially loves telling a chilling ghost story while nestled beside a bonfire.